Jan...

From Norm & Luann Rhode -
Dodge City, Kansas July 11, 1992

SENTINEL TO THE CIMARRON: THE FRONTIER EXPERIENCE OF FORT DODGE, KANSAS

By

DAVID KAY STRATE

Cultural Heritage and Arts Center

Dodge City, Kansas

Cultural Heritage and Arts Center

Title III, ESEA — Project No. 68-5772

Dodge City U. S. D. No. 443

Dodge City, Kansas

July 1970

Library of Congress Number: 74-127192

The work presented or reported herein was performed pursuant to a Grant from the U. S. Office of Education, Department of Health, Education, and Welfare. However, the opinions expressed herein do not necessarily reflect the position or policy of the U. S. Office of Education, and no official endorsement by the U. S. Office of Education should be inferred.

Cover by Dave Harris
from a painting by Olaf Seltzer, with the gracious permission of the Thomas Gilcrease Institute of American History and Art, Tulsa

Printed in the United States
High Plains Publishers, Inc.
Dodge City, Kansas

To The Family

For Hands Along the Way

PREFACE

This book is a study of the establishment and service of Fort Dodge, Kansas, from 1865 until 1882. Examination of the wealth of available published material concerning the expansion of the military frontier through the Central Plains indicates that the history of this post has largely been neglected.

Following the closing of the fort in 1882 several years lapsed before a second mission was found for the facilities which remained. In 1890 Fort Dodge was re-opened as a state soldier's home to accommodate Kansas veterans. Because the military function of Fort Dodge was found to be quite different from the post's later use as a soldier's home, an epilogue has been added, whereby this phase of Fort Dodge's years of service is considered separately.

Because the first years of the fort were closely paralleled by the growth of the Kansas settler's frontier, considerable attention has been given to the latter. In addition to Fort Dodge's responsibility to the settler a second task was given to the post. This task was that of guarding the Santa Fe Trail and the Smoky Hill Route, both of which were primary commercial routes across the Central Plains.

The author is deeply indebted to routine practices of the United States Army by which a thorough record of post activities was kept. Without the wealth of records relative to Fort Dodge which have been preserved by the National Archives, no comprehensive reconstruction of the post's history would be possible. Included in these records are Medical Records, Letters Sent 1866-1882, Telegrams Received 1874, Reports and Journals of Scouts and Marches 1866-1882, Special Orders 1866-1882, Consolidated Quartermaster Correspondence and Orders and General Orders 1866-1882.

All of these records were made available to the author on micro-film by Mr. Arthur Rose, Superintendent of the Kansas State Soldier's Home at Fort Dodge. Mr. Rose and his staff were most helpful and considerate during the many months required to complete the task of examining these holdings.

Mr. Nyle Miller, Secretary of the Kansas State Historical Society at Topeka, and Mr. Joseph Snell, Assistant Archivist of the Kansas State Historical Society were most helpful during the period of research. Both gentlemen made every effort to locate and make available all of the society's records on the post to the author. The Governor's Papers, part of which cover the years of Fort Dodge's service, proved to be of considerable value in gathering the mosaic pieces of the fort's history.

The staff personnel of the Oklahoma State University Library, University of Wyoming Library, Wichita State University Library, Kansas City Public Library, Dodge City Public Library, St. Mary of the Plains College Library and the Wichita Public Library were all most helpful in assisting the author's search for rare editions that were of significant value to the final book. The author is also indebted to Sister M. Grace Schonlau, Ph.D., who read the first drafts for language construction errors.

The author also acknowledges his debt of appreciation to Dr. Norbert Mahnken, Dr. Theodore Agnew, Dr. Homer Knight, Dr. Robert Alciatore and Dr. Walter Scott of the Oklahoma State University graduate faculty who served on the doctoral committee during the thesis stage of this book. A final measure of gratitude is extended to Jane R. Robison, Director of the Cultural Heritage and Arts Center at Dodge City, Kansas and her staff for their collective effort to bring this work to publication. Working under the auspices of the U. S. Department of Health, Education and Welfare, Washington, D. C., they have performed a yeoman task in preserving and enriching the unique yesteryear of frontier Kansas.

—David K. Strate

TABLE OF CONTENTS

ILLUSTRATIONS

MAPS

INTRODUCTION

The history of Fort Dodge is closely wedded to both the frontier experience of Kansas and the growing commercial arteries which crossed that state to serve the entire nation. The commercial frontier reached and spanned the prairies of Kansas by 1821, approximately three decades prior to the arrival of the settler's frontier.[1] Both of these frontiers were exposed to numerous elements of hardship and violence within the geographical confines of that area which was to be formed into the State of Kansas in 1861.

The process of penetration, exploration and settlement which followed in the wake of European discovery of the new Western Hemisphere scarcely touched the Great Plains before the area was transferred to the United States by France as part of the Louisiana Purchase of 1803. Spanish treks across the plains in search of fabled wealth uncovered nothing more attractive than huge expanses of semi-arid prairie and primitive native villages. Perhaps the introduction of Christianity to the area and the establishment of widely scattered missions and settlements along the southern borders of the plains afforded minimal solace to the Spaniards, but their primary objective of locating reservoirs of wealth in the form of precious metals was soon abandoned.

If the exploration of this territory proved disappointing to the Spanish, it was a windfall for the natives that peopled the plains. Spain had introduced a vital instrument for the eventual maturation of the Plains Indian culture. The horse proved to be ideal for locating and preying on the huge herds of bison which roamed the plains.[2] The cultural warp effected on the Indians by the introduction of the horse was to have a profound effect on the final contest for possession of the plains which was fought from 1862 until 1878, between the U. S. Army and the "Lords of the Plains."

The lapse of in excess of three centuries between the introduction of the horse by the Spanish in 1541, and the outbreak of the Plains Wars in 1862, had given the Indian the time needed to become expert in the adaptation of the horse to warfare.[3] The native cavalrymen met by the wagonmaster and the soldier on the plains of Kansas proved to be a most formidable and resourceful adversary.

The penetration of the plains by the United States followed quickly on the heels of President Jefferson's successful negotiations to obtain France's Louisiana holdings. Lewis and Clark's expedition, from 1804 to 1806, was immediately followed by a frontier vanguard of traders and trappers, who soon developed lucrative markets with the Indians.[4] There was the promise of even greater returns if the area's natural wealth could be exploited without hindrance from the natives.

Captain William Becknell's successful expedition in 1821, demonstrated the feasibility of crossing the plains to trade with Mexico.[5] The volume of goods carried by pack mules and wagon train grew dramatically during the years which followed Becknell's initial venture. By 1826, the trade had become reciprocal as enterprising Mexican merchants, following the cue of their American counterparts along the Missouri River, sought to share in the newly discovered wealth of prairie commerce.[6]

The strategic central location and easily negotiable topographical features of the Kansas plains were readily utilized by several of the nation's most vital commercial routes.[7] This area possessed two of the West's finest natural river valley highways. The Santa Fe Trail stretched southwestward from its eastern terminus of Kansas City, Missouri, until it reached central Kansas. The later Smoky Hill Route ran from Leavenworth, Kansas, to Denver, Colorado, parallel to the state's northern border.

At this point the route met the Great Bend of the Arkansas River. Here the trail continued southward along the north bank of the river until the fording area at the Cimarron Crossing was reached in western Kansas.[8] The majority of the wagons traveling this route turned southwestward again, after having forded the river, along the Cimarron Cutoff toward their eventual destination of Santa Fe.[9]

As the returns from these capitalistic ventures grew, major companies, such as that of Russell, Majors and Waddell, were soon sending thousands of wagons onto the plains each year. Thieves and Indians soon appeared to challenge the wagonmaster for the goods he carried, and violence became a constant companion of the emerging commercial frontier. These marauders were immediately drawn to the Santa Fe Trail, and the frequent success of their attacks forced the sponsors of the trains to appeal to the government for protection.[10]

It was essential that a nation such as the United States, chronically faced with a shortage of specie and an unfavorable balance of trade, should guard such a valuable artery of bullion entry as that provided by the Santa Fe Trail, yet the problem of effecting adequate protection would prove most vexing. The route between Council Grove and Santa Fe extended over approximately 800 miles of territory that was almost entirely unpopulated except for roaming bands of Plains Indians.

Of the two alternatives available to the military for providing some measure of protection along the trail, that of sending detachments of troops down the trail on punitive expeditions from military posts near the eastern terminus of the route or of establishing minor military posts, manned by small detachments, at strategic points along the entire route, neither proved to be entirely satisfactory.[11] Marauding bands of Indians retired before the challenge of a superior force, usually choosing to attack public trains or small military units rather than to risk the chance of a major defeat. As soon as a sizable military force had withdrawn in frustration, the Indians were free to continue their attacks on less dangerous prey.

As the decade of the 1840's wore on, Mexico undoubtedly regretted her decision to participate in the trade carried over the Santa Fe Route. The rapid growth of economic rapport between the two nations accentuated the desirability of drafting a formal commercial treaty. However, the Mexican government refused to invite further encroachment by their ambitious northern neighbor by bowing to such an agreement.[12] The continued deterioration of Mexican-American relations forced the government of the United States to consider the importance of the trail if war should break out, yet the question of the method of protecting the route was for the time being largely settled by circumstances.

The establishment of a series of posts along the route was postponed as the nation's military resources were drawn up for the coming contest with Mexico. A second crisis, that of the Civil War, continued this postponement until 1865, when the nation could again give proper attention to the problem of guarding the frontier.[13]

Perhaps the most vulnerable location for attacks on trains moving over the Santa Fe Trail was at the Cimarron Crossing of the Arkansas River.[14] This site had initially served as a favorite rendezvous point for mountain trappers after the Arkansas River west of the Great Bend had become a portion of the United States' western international boundary with Spain by the provisions of the Adams-Onis Treaty of 1819. The Cimarron soon became a sizable camping and trading ground, which was used at various times by mountain men, traders, wagon trains, military detachments and Indians.[15]

Wagon trains usually rested for several days at the Cimarron before continuing on. Indians, drawn to the camp sites to trade and beg, often attacked these trains during the process of fording, when they were most vulnerable. Even large, well armed trains could be overrun if the attack was timed to fall on the travelers while their numbers were split by the waters of the river.[16]

In response to the growing frequency of these attacks, Fort Mann, in reality a way station, was established near this point of the Cimarron in 1845.[17] The military significance of the post must be considered to have been quite modest. The fortifications of the post consisted of nothing more than four log houses set in a square and connected by log walls twenty feet high and sixty feet long.[18] The log houses of Fort Mann could garrison only a small detachment of troops; however, travelers along the route welcomed the opportunity to rest, to repair their equipment, and to trade tired or disabled draft animals for rested stock previously exchanged by an earlier train, without the threat of attack on the open prairie.

Lieutenant George D. Brewerton, who commanded a small detachment of army guards that were traveling the Santa Fe Trail with a government train during the Mexican War, gave the following description of Fort Mann's garrison:

> Upon the day following the passage of the Arkansas, we halted near Mann's Fort, a little government post, or half-way depot, then garrisoned

by a handful of volunteers who drank corn whiskey, consumed Uncle Sam's bacon and hard tack, drew their pay with undeviating regularity, and otherwise wore out their lives in the service of their country. In the meantime these doughty warriors dispelled their ennui by chasing buffalo, or sallying forth to scout up and down, with a general understanding that they were to quarrel with the Comanches if they could catch them — a combination of circumstances which as it requires two parties to make a bargain, occurred but seldom.[19]

The volume of goods passing Fort Mann increased dramatically during the course of the Mexican War as the military wrestled with the problem of supplying large armies in the field over several thousand miles of difficult terrain.[20] During 1848, the war with Mexico ended, and the sharp reduction in government trains which accompanied peace led to the abandonment of the fort in 1850, when a new post, Fort Atkinson, was established six miles down stream.[21]

Unlike Fort Mann, which had served the needs of public and commercial trains to a much greater extent than chastizing marauding Indians, Fort Atkinson was intended to function primarily as a traditional military installation; yet the life of this new post was unusually short. The frequency of Indian attack on travelers of the Santa Fe Trail declined sharply during the following years, and the post was abandoned in 1853.[22]

This decision proved to be short sighted in the light of events that struck the territory in the years that lay immediately ahead. The sectional dispute between the North and the South over slavery grew increasingly heated, and Congress's passage of Senator Stephen Douglas's ill-fated Kansas-Nebraska Act in 1854, with its provision of popular sovereignty, brought the slavery contest directly to Kansas after it had been granted territorial status that same year. The clash of abolitionists and the advocates of slavery convulsed the territory for several years before Kansas was admitted into the Union as a free state in 1861.

As the Civil War was drawing to a close, Major General Grenville M. Dodge, commanding officer of the Department of the Missouri, issued an order to Brigadier General James H. Ford, commanding officer of the District of the Upper Arkansas, on March 18, 1865, to establish a new post on or near the old site of Fort Atkinson.[23] By early April crude earth dugouts had been fashioned along the north banks of the Arkansas River, and troops had arrived to man the modest fortifications of Fort Dodge.[24]

The officers and enlisted men who served at the fort from 1865 until 1882, were subjected to unusual hardship and deprivation. The isolation of the post was almost complete. The settler's frontier did not reach Fort Dodge until 1872, and the fortification's nearest sister post, Fort Larned, lay in excess of fifty miles northeastward across the open expanses of the rolling prairie of western Kansas.

The sources of limestone and timber needed to replace the earth dugouts with permanent buildings and corrals were separated from the post by from ten to twelve miles of prairie.[25] The difficult task of quarrying stone and sawing timber to be hauled to the post for construction and kindling was compounded by the constant threat of Indian attack on work details sent out from the post.

During the first two years of the fort's existence, there was the distinct possibility that the garrison would be overrun and annihilated by surrounding Plains Indians, who were alarmed at the strategic location of the fortification near the fording area of the Cimarron.[26] The plain food, exacting labor, lack of diversion and hazardous field duty experienced by the troops of the Fort Dodge command led many to choose desertion rather than to continue soldiering on the plains.[27]

The assistance rendered by Fort Dodge to the expanding frontier was significant, yet it has been largely overlooked in the process of shaping the pattern of American military history. The men of the post were involved in scouts, marches and campaigns almost continually from 1865 until 1878. Weary cavalrymen often found that they had ridden in excess of fifteen hundred miles during a single season while guarding the Kansas frontier.[28] From 1867 until 1874, the fort was involved in several major campaigns to eliminate the menace of Indian depredations on the plains. By 1882, the last threat of Indian attack on the settlements of Kansas had been removed, and the post was no longer considered necessary to the defense of the frontier. On October second of that year, the last troops to garrison Fort Dodge were ordered south to Camp Supply in the Indian Territory, and a vital facet of the nation's frontier history had been completed.[29]

The SANTA FE TRAIL
Colorado
Kansas
Mo.
Ark.
Oklahoma
Texas
New Mexico
Missouri River
Kaw River
Osage River
Neosho River
Arkansas R.
Arkansas River
North Canadian River
Cimarron River
Canadian River
Purgatoire R.
Rio Grande River
Pecos River
MOUNTAIN BRANCH
CIMARRON CUTOFF
SANGRE DE CRISTO MOUNTAINS
SPANISH PEAKS
OLD FRANKLIN
BOONVILLE
ARROW ROCK
FORT OSAGE
WESTPORT
INDEPENDENCE
FORT LEAVENWORTH
OREGON TRAIL
SHAWNEE MISSION
GARDNER
OREGON TRAIL JUNCTION
BURLINGAME
COUNCIL GROVE
DIAMOND SPRINGS
LYONS
FORT ZARAH
GREAT BEND
PAWNEE ROCK
FORT LARNED
LARNED
DODGE CITY
FORT DODGE
CACHES
CIMARRON
CHOUTEAUS ISLAND UPPER CROSSING
FORT AUBREY
ULYSSES
LOWER SPRINGS
MIDDLE SPRING
POINT OF ROCK
LAMAR
BENTS NEW FORT
FORT WISE, FT. LYON NO. 1
FORT LYONS NO 2
LAS ANIMAS
BENTS OLD FORT
LA JUNTA
PUEBLO
TRINIDAD
RATON PASS
RATON
CLIFTON HOUSE
CIMARRON
RAYADO
TAOS
OCATE CROSSING
FORT UNION
LA JUNTA (WATROUS)
LAS VAGAS
SAN MIGUEL
PECOS RUINS
GLORIETTA PASS
SANTA FE
UPPER SPRING
COLD SPRING
BOISE CITY
POINT OF ROCK
MCNEES CROSSING
CAMP NICHOLS
RABBIT EARS
RABBIT EAR CREEK CAMP
CLAYTON
CANADIAN CROSSING
ROUND MOUND
WAGON MOUND
Rock or Carrizo Cr.
Ute Cr.
200
100
50
25
0
Drawn by Frank A. Cooper
Mrs. Frank A. Cooper
Santa Fe Trail Highway Association

CHAPTER I

THE KANSAS FRONTIER, 1840 TO 1865: A CRUCIBLE OF VIOLENCE

Gilpin's Volunteers

As the Mexican War drew to a close, the government rather tardily turned its attention to the problem of guarding the Santa Fe Trail. Missouri merchants, who were being threatened with financial ruin as a result of losses sustained during raids, demanded that the military remove the Indian menace along the route.

The Department of War responded on August 20, 1847, by authorizing Governor John C. Edwards of Missouri, to raise a punitive expedition from among the returning Missouri veterans of the Mexican War.[1] Lieutenant Colonel William Gilpin was placed in command and authorized to gather five companies of men. To Gilpin's dismay, few returning veterans chose to enlist for a second expedition so quickly after returning home from the Mexican conflict. Most of those who did enlist were German immigrants from the St. Louis area. Few of these men had any formal military experience and many of them could not speak English.[2]

During the winter of 1847, Colonel Gilpin's volunteers garrisoned at Fort Mann, near the Cimarron on the Arkansas River. The Colonel had orders to conclude treaties with as many of the Plains Indian tribes as possible, but in the event of their refusal to make peace, he was to engage them in combat in the field. Although he failed to secure treaties with any of the plains tribes, Colonel Gilpin considered his poorly trained and undisciplined troops unfit for an assault on the Indians, and he brought his command back to St. Louis in August of 1848.[3]

The most significant contribution of the expedition was Colonel Gilpin's recommendation to the Secretary of War that several adobe posts be built along the course of the trail rather than to use military expeditions from Fort Leavenworth, as had earlier been recommended by General Philip Kearny.[4] Although the Santa Fe Trail was to remain poorly guarded until after the conclusion of the Civil War, Colonel Gilpin's suggestions found immediate favor with the War Department, and plans were drawn up for the eventual establishment of the recommended series of forts.

The Crisis over Slavery

The second plague of violence visited on the territory was ushered in by the settler's frontier rather than the commercial frontier. The uneasy truce that had been established between the advocates and opponents of slavery by the Missouri Compromise of 1820 was no longer viable as Kansas approached territorial status. The admission of Texas in 1845 and the Treaty of Guadalupe Hidalgo in 1848, following the Mexican War, had added huge expanses of territory to the American Southwest.

Abolitionists demanded an end to the extension of slavery into new territory, while the advocates of black servitude were equally vocal in their insistence that it was the prerogative of the people within the territories to be formed into states to continue the institution of slavery if they so chose. The Compromise of 1850 permitted a choice on the question of slavery to the inhabitants of all the territory annexed from Mexico except California, which was admitted as a free state. However, the issue of slavery, far from being settled, was merely deferred until 1861.

During the 1850's the settler's frontier pressed steadily westward into the Kansas and Nebraska Territories. The Kansas-Nebraska Act of 1854 repealed the slave-restricting provision of the Missouri Compromise from the remaining territory of the Louisiana Purchase, thereby ushering in a violent contest in the newly formed Territory of Kansas.

The savagery of the struggle that followed between the forces of abolitionism and slavery drew the attention of the entire nation, but it was largely Kansas that suffered. Groups of para-military ruffians roamed the territory leaving death and ruin in their wake.[5] Outlaw bands, with little or no sentiment regarding the slavery question, utilized the struggle to excuse their assaults on frontier settlements. Abolitionists usually attributed these attacks to Missouri invaders they referred to as "bushwhackers," while the proslave elements swore these acts were the work of the fanatic opponents of black servitude.[6] Many demoralized settlers who had been caught up in the struggle left the territory rather than risk death or financial ruin at the hands of these bands.[7]

Political opportunists in search of public office and private fortune entered the territory in increasing numbers during the difficult years of the late 1850's.[8] As the political structure of Kansas deteriorated steadily, the incidence of fraud by those in public office rose. Indian agents were frequently charged with profiteering from the indiscriminate sale of firearms to the Plains Indians.[9] Attempts by public officials to dispose fraudulently of Indian lands and the toleration of squatters on reservations eroded still further the territory's already strained relations with the Indians.[10]

Once the pattern of political instability and violence had become entrenched, it was not easily eliminated. The deep scar of civil disorder lingered to trouble the public body of Kansas throughout the course of the Civil War and, in some areas of the state, well into the 1870's.[11] The later gunslingers of such cattle towns as Wichita, Abilene and Dodge City had often received their schooling in the art of killing during these difficult years.

Kansas and the Civil War

The people of Kansas were granted no respite when the contest over slavery finally reached the proportions of a national civil war in 1861. Having entered the Union that same year as a free state, Kansas was soon asked to meet federal troop quotas. Conscription was never necessary within Kansas.[12] The citizens of the state had endured informal war for several years, and they were perhaps relieved to see the struggle move toward a final climax.

The ranks of the state's newly created battalions were usually filled within days after the call for enlistment had been sent out. Although Kansas played a rather minor part in the outcome of the Civil War, she sustained the highest per-capita losses of any state in the Union.[13] Kansas battalions of Indians, Negroes and whites served with distinction in several campaigns during the course of the war.

In 1861, General James H. Lane and Colonel Charles R. Jennison led raids into western Missouri. The town of Osceola was sacked by Kansas troops on September 23.[14] This action invited reprisal, and General Sterling Price responded immediately by leading his army of Missourians into eastern Kansas on the heels of Lane's withdrawal from Missouri. General Price's attack on Kansas closely resembled General Lane's action in Missouri. After he had revenged Osceola by desolating several border communities, he retreated into Missouri.[15]

This early action was characteristic of the border skirmishes carried on between these states throughout the course of the Civil War. Although a sustained invasion of Kansas was never successful, both the eastern and southern borders of the state were periodically menaced by Confederate troops. In 1864, the Confederacy moved units from Texas as far north as the Canadian River, on the southwestern border of Kansas; but they returned to Texas without giving battle as Kansas volunteer units massed near the border to receive the expected attack.[16]

The Unguarded Frontier

Although the Plains Indians' assault on the settlements and commercial routes of Kansas did not reach a climax until the late years of the Civil War, the frequency of attack had increased steadily throughout the state's territorial years from 1854 through 1861. The volunteer battalions required by Kansas to guard her borders from Confederate invasion sapped the state's meager reservoir of available manpower. This situation placed the frontier settlements of the northern and western areas of the state in the position of being almost entirely without military assistance to ward off the increasing number of Indian depredations which were committed throughout the course of the war.[17]

The most troublesome tribes were the Kiowas and the Comanches, who hunted South of the Arkansas River, and the Cheyennes and Arapahoes, who roamed the High Plains north from the Arkansas to the Platte River of the Nebraska Territory.[18] These tribes had observed that the clamor of travel along the Santa Fe Trail had drastically reduced the numbers of buffalo available for hunting purposes. They were also concerned with the encroachment of the frontier on several sites on the plains of Kansas, which held unusual religious significance for them. A number of the plains tribes made annual pilgrimages to the Republican and Solomon Valleys to make "medicine" which would insure their success while hunting and provide them with protection from their enemies.[19]

Travelers along the Santa Fe Trail had noted that Indians frequently gathered at Pawnee Rock, an incongruous outcropping of earth and stone on the Kansas central plains, to perform religious ceremonies.[20] The preoccupation of Kansans with the slavery question provided these tribes with what they considered to be an ideal opportunity to close the Santa Fe Trail and to push the settler's frontier eastward through a series of attacks along the frontier.

The number and seriousness of these depredations grew rapidly after the Indians found that their initial attacks brought only token attempts at reprisal by federal troops or Kansas militia. Fort Larned was the only military post within the state that was situated west of Fort Riley. This post had been established along the Santa Fe Trail in 1859, approximately two hundred miles west of Fort Riley on the Pawnee Fork of the Arkansas River.[21] Only three companies of troops could be garrisoned at Fort Larned, a fact which seriously reduced the capacity of the post to punish marauding bands of Indians.

Public Demands for Protection

As spokesmen for the people, the newspapers of Kansas became increasingly insistent that positive measures be taken to stop these assaults on the frontier. Each fresh attack brought a detailed account of the crime along with heated suggestions for the final settlement of the Indian problem. The *Smoky Hill and Republican Union* offered the following solace to its readers:

> THE INDIANS — Our "red brethren" still show unpleasant signs of "obstropulousness." The Pawnees do nothing but steal, never did do anything but steal, and never will do anything but steal. Stealing is undoubtedly their "forte" — they take to it as a hog does to a mud puddle — as Rum takes a fellow to the devil. It is, indeed, dear reader, charmingly interesting to be possessed of a good horse, and have a band of these roving neighbors in the settlement. In fact, our "brethern" seem aware of the truth that the Jayhawkers are played out and upon the strength of that are evidently trying to "run the machine" themselves. Their success is perfect — a little more so than is agreeable. It illustrates, however, their precociousness; the remarkable adaptibility of their nature to anything that is "fancy," "fast" — fast horses for instance. But we didn't start out particularly with the intention of analyzing their character — suffice it to say they haven't got any —.[22]

The *Western Journal of Commerce* suggested, rather facetiously, that President Lincoln and Secretary of War Stanton consider drafting Indians into the army to remove them from the frontier. The editor noted that there were perhaps ten thousand braves around Fort Larned who had demonstrated on numerous occasions their desire to fight by threatening to take the post.[23] Stage coaches traveling over the Santa Fe Trail frequently arrived at their destination with members of the crew and passengers killed or wounded and with the coach filled with bullet holes and protruding arrows.[24] They often brought with them the bodies of settlers found dead near their route of travel.

The loss of horses and mules to raiding bands was at times so heavy that travel and mail service were suspended until the animals could be replaced.[25] Militia units were often hastily formed from the limited reservoir of manpower available, but they proved incapable of adequately defending the state's western lines of mail and commerce. As the financial losses sustained by companies using the Santa Fe Trail grew, stage travel was at first reduced and then finally suspended altogether until sufficient protection could be provided.[26]

The Road to the Chivington Massacre

The Territory of Colorado shared with Kansas the experience of frequent attacks by Indians along her frontier. The discovery of gold at Cherry Creek, in 1858, had initiated a rush by hopeful miners over the Kansas routes and had alarmed the Plains Indians.[27] The depredations committed against settlements and mining camps in Colorado became so intense in the spring of 1864 that Governor John Evans ordered Colonel John Chivington and his command of Third Colorado Volunteers into the field on a punitive campaign.[28]

Colonel Chivington sent Lieutenant George S. Eayre and one company of troops into northwestern Kansas to seek out and attack Indians. On May 16, Lieutenant Eayre engaged a band of Cheyennes under Chief Black Kettle and Lean Bear approximately fifty miles northwest of Fort Larned.[29] The lieutenant's casualties included four killed and three wounded. He estimated that his troops had killed or wounded perhaps ten of the Indians. Following this skirmish Lieutenant Eayre immediately gave up the field to the Indians and marched his command to Fort Larned, undoubtedly persuading his adversaries that they had been attacked by troops from that post.[30]

The response to Lieutenant Eayre's engagement was a furious assault on the Kansas frontier, with Fort Larned as the focal point of the attack. One hundred and eight government horses were taken by the Indians from the garrison in July while they were grazing near the post.[31] The ranches west of Fort Larned on Walnut Creek were burned out and at least ten men were killed.[32] As a result of the Cheyennes' success, the Arapahoes and Kiowas also took to the warpath. In an effort to stop these assaults, Governor Thomas Carney of Kansas sent General James Blunt westward with a hastily assembled battalion of Kansas militia. Blunt moved his command to the vicinity of Fort Larned, where three public trains had been attacked and all their stock lost. There he engaged an estimated fifteen hundred warriors near the Pawnee Fork of the Arkansas River and succeeded in killing nine of their number.[33] The devastation of the Kansas frontier observed by Blunt on his march westward persuaded him no peace should be offered to the Plains Indians until they had first been severely punished for their atrocities.[34]

The assaults on the outlying settlements of Kansas pushed the western frontier steadily eastward, thereby exposing to attack entire towns that had previously been situated safely within the frontier's protective perimeter. On August 16, 1864, Marysville, Kansas, located north of Topeka, was attacked and seventeen citizens of the town lost their lives.[35] The Cheyennes and Sioux who were involved in the assault had become so sophisticated in the art of warfare that they were supported in the field by supplies they carried on previously captured wagons and by several hundred head of livestock they had gathered to feed on as they moved eastward.[36]

Major Edward W. Wyncoop, who was in command at Fort Lyon, Colorado Territory, and also served as agent to the Cheyennes, worked diligently to restore peace to the Kansas and Colorado frontiers. The Major persuaded William Bent to mediate with the Cheyennes and Arapahoes, but Governor Evans of Colorado refused to treat with the tribes until they had been punished for their attacks.[37]

Governor Evans responded to Major Wyncoop's offer of mediation by ordering Colonel Chivington to press the attack on the offenders as quickly as possible. Colonel Chivington's force was composed largely of men who had witnessed first hand the depredations of the Indians along the frontier.[38] As the period of enlistment of the command was for only one hundred days, the Colonel knew he must strike immediately or the men would be discharged.

The climax of the year's struggle on the plains was reached at dawn on November 29, 1864, when Colonel Chivington's troops attacked Chief Black Kettle's band of Cheyennes at Sand Creek. One hundred sixty-three Cheyennes were killed during Colonel Chivington's charge, one hundred and ten of which were women and children.[39] Some of the men of the command committed atrocities against the persons of the Cheyennes that were equally as brutal as those perpetrated by the Indians along the frontier. Scalps were taken and the bodies of a number of the slain Cheyennes were multilated. Several of Colonel Chivington's men took parts of corpses back to Denver as evidence of their victory.[40]

Approximately two hundred settlers and travelers in Kansas had lost their lives through Indian attacks during the year 1864.[41] It was not possible to tabulate the number of Indians killed during the same period, but with the heavy toll taken by Colonel Chivington, it most certainly exceeded that of the whites.

The Debate over the Indian Problem

The storm of criticism which had been building steadily in the East over the government's handling of the Indian problem reached new heights when the news of the Chivington Massacre was received. Colonel Chivington and the men of the Third Colorado Volunteers escaped punishment only because their terms of enlistment expired before court martial hearings could be convened.[42] The Senate passed a bill which would have suspended the pay of command, but the House of Representatives failed to muster enough votes to sustain this action.[43]

It was perhaps to be expected that as the country tabulated the awesome cost in lives and ruin experienced during the first years of the Civil War a strong protest would be lodged against the apparently unnecessary bloodshed that was taking place concurrently on the plains. In general, the people of Kansas were puzzled by what appeared to them to be unrealistic Eastern obstinacy. They demanded that thorough retaliatory measures be taken and that no peace treaties be made until the Indians demonstrated a willingness to abide permanently by them.

The *Western Journal of Commerce* offered the following suggestions to opponents of punishment:

> Peace with the Indians of the Plains
>
> The New York and other eastern journals are lamenting the oppression of the Government upon the unoffending aborigines who have been indulging in a little "misunderstanding" with us on the western plains. These eastern people who have acquired their knowledge of Indian character from the speeches of "Logan" and other school book publications are deprecating any farther war upon the nobles of the tomahawk and scalping knife.
>
> We do not believe that the people of the Great West are more blood thirsty or less humane, than the dwellers under the benignities of Eastern civilization; and it is a libel upon the army of the West, to intimate that they are murdering the Indians merely to show that they are not idle.
>
> It might straighten the vision of some of these cross-eyed editors to be scalped a few times. We would advise a trip across the plains as a thorough curative to all such school girl sentiment about the savages who have visited upon the peaceful white inhabitant of the West, all the horrors of Indian warfare for the last eighteen months.[44]

Although the men and supplies for a full scale campaign against the Plains Indians in Kansas were not yet available because of the priority given to the Civil War campaigns, the magnitude of the attacks committed on the frontier during 1864 forced the government to take some measure of positive action. The intensity of the Indians assault on Fort Larned and the area immediately surrounding the post necessitated the building of sister posts close by.

Fort Harker was established in August, 1864, on the north bank of the Smoky Hill River at the point where the Santa Fe stage road turned southward to meet the Great Bend of the Arkansas River.[45] Fort Zarah was established in September, 1864, on the east bank of Walnut Creek near the junction of that stream with the Arkansas River.[46] The strategic positioning of these posts near the site of Fort Larned provided an added measure of protection to the settlers and travelers of west central Kansas, but the task of building posts to watch over western Kansas was postponed until the following year.

The Dodge Campaign of 1865

In December, 1864, Major General Grenville M. Dodge was placed in command of the Department of the Missouri, and in January of the following year the old Department of Kansas was merged into the General's district.[47] This consolidation of military departments brought all of the plains territory from the Arkansas River of southern Kansas northward to the Yellowstone River of the Montana Territory under his authority.

Dodge, an engineer by profession, had been commissioned a Major General in July, 1863, and placed in General William T. Sherman's command. He had supervised the restoration of railroads in Georgia in support of Sherman's Atlanta Campaign until he was wounded in August of that year near Roswell, Georgia.[48] In January, 1865, General Grant ordered Dodge to Fort Leavenworth to plan a punitive campaign against the Plains Indians.[49]

The general was appalled by the reports which reached him upon his arrival at Fort Leavenworth. Dodge had two detachments of troops at his disposal, the Eleventh and Sixteenth Kansas Cavalry regiments; however, the discipline and morale of the troops left much to be desired.[50] The small detachments garrisoning the posts along the Santa Fe and Smoky Hill Routes refused to leave the protection of their stockades.[51] During the previous summer they had been beaten by the Indians in nearly every engagement.

Stage lines had abandoned travel across the plains, and most of the telegraph lines had been destroyed. The people who remained in western Kansas and southern Nebraska were without mail and in a state of general panic. Dodge considered almost every tribe from Texas to the Yellowstone to be on the warpath, largely in response to the successes of the Kiowas, Comanches, Cheyennes and Arapahoes on the plains of Kansas during the preceding summer.[52]

The general immediately ordered the two Kansas regiments under his command to march to Fort Kearny to relieve the settlers under attack along the Smoky Hill and South Platte Routes and to restore the lines of communication that had been torn down. Initially the officers of his command refused to order their men into the field during the grip of an unusually harsh winter, but the order was finally obeyed after Dodge threatened to court-martial any officer who failed to ready his men for the march.[53]

Scouts who had been sent onto the plains to locate warring bands of Indians reported the presence of a large number of licensed traders who were selling contraband guns and ammunition to the Indians at exorbitant prices. The general revoked all permits to trade and ordered his officers to arrest all traders found with Indian or government stock.[54]

On the march to Fort Kearny during early February Dodge lost thirteen men from frostbite, and the entire command suffered considerably from exposure.[55] The Indians steadily refused to engage the command in a major contest, but frequent skirmishes occurred over the course of the long march. Those Indians who were in the path of Dodge's march moved either southward or northward to escape punishment. As the telegraph lines were repaired and news was sent eastward that the route had been opened, travelers again ventured onto the plains.[56]

Upon reaching Fort Kearny, General Dodge was advised that the Santa Fe Trail was being menaced by Indians who had fled southward to avoid his command. The general considered the Indians' grip on the plains to be broken and returned to Fort Leavenworth, after ordering Brevet Major General James H. Ford southward to relieve the remaining pressure along the Arkansas River.[57] On Ford's arrival in western Kansas, the Indians again refused engagement and moved further southward into the Wichita Mountains of the Indian Territory. He repeated Dodge's process of repairing the lines of communication and then moved his troops back to Fort Larned for the remainder of the winter.[58]

Although these winter marches had temporarily forced the Indians to abandon the plains between the Platte and Arkansas Rivers, Dodge realized that the accomplishments of the campaign were modest and that spring would undoubtedly bring a fresh wave of Indian attacks to this same area of the plains. On his return to Fort Leavenworth, he immediately commenced planning for a two-pronged spring campaign into the territory he had covered the past winter.

Dodge intended to lead the northern campaign personally against the Northern Cheyennes, Arapahoes and several bands of Sioux, who had raided southward into Kansas and Nebraska the previous year before returning to the Black Hills. The southern campaign was to be under the command of Ford. His task was to move southwestward from Fort Larned toward the Cimarron and to engage any Indians that he contacted along the route of march. On reaching the Cimarron he was to cross over the Arkansas River and proceed southward, punishing those bands of Apaches, Southern Cheyennes, Arapahoes, Kiowas and Comanches that had raided in Kansas almost continually during the summers of 1863 and 1864.[59]

General Ford's Abortive Arkansas River Campaign

On his return to Fort Larned, Ford immediately commenced preparations for the forthcoming spring campaign. He was ordered by the Department of the Missouri to retain two companies of the Eleventh Kansas Cavalry at Fort Larned and to place the remaining companies enroute to Fort Leavenworth, where they were to join the troops being gathered there for the northern army which was to campaign in the Black Hills.[60]

By mid-February, news of Dodge's winter march had reached the East, and a new barrage of condemnation relative to the government's handling of the Indian problem quickly followed. Almost simultaneously, Colonel Jesse Leavenworth, United States Indian Agent to the tribes south of the Arkansas River, received word that Ford was preparing to take the field in the spring. He responded by notifying the general that he had recently held council with the leading chiefs of the Arapahoes, Kiowas and Apaches and had presented them with gifts from the government.[61] In return, he had received their assurance that they wanted permanent peace and would not again attack the travelers of the Santa Fe Trail or raid the settlements of western Kansas.

Leavenworth requested that the general keep his command north of the Arkansas River until a formal treaty could be written with the Indians under his jurisdiction. Ford conveyed the request to Dodge, who advised him that his duty was to punish them and that he should continue his preparations for the spring campaign.[62]

The most vexing problem faced by Ford in readying his troops for the field was that of securing suitable mounts. As a veteran of plains campaigning, he knew that by April the ponies ridden by the Indian would again be feeding on green grass and that excellent mounts would have to be secured for his command if they were to be successful in pursuing and engaging the Indians. Horses brought from the East often required several months of conditioning before they were suitable for sustained marches.[63]

The general anticipated taking only cavalry into the field, while leaving his infantry to garrison Fort Larned. His troops were to be supplied with no subsistence rations other than parched corn mixed with sugar and a few days' supply of flour.[64] Buffalo meat was to make up the bulk of the diet during the march. By traveling light he hoped to keep his troops in the field for from thirty to sixty days, constantly pressing the Indians, thereby forcing them to stand and fight as often as he could.[65]

On March 17, Ford's scouts brought back reports that approximately two thousand Comanche warriors, as well as several bands of Apaches and Kiowas, were camped on the Cimarron River.[66] They estimated that an additional eight hundred Arapahoes were gathered on Crooked Creek, twenty miles south of the Comanche encampment.[67] Ford immediately relayed this report to Dodge, who ordered him to establish a new post at or near the site of old Fort Atkinson. By March 20 an engineer had been sent from Fort Leavenworth to assist in laying out the new post.[68]

Later that same month General Ford ordered Captain Henry Pearce to proceed, with Company C of the Eleventh Kansas Cavalry, to the recommended site and to commence erection of the fort. Pearce considered the site of Fort Atkinson to be indefensible and on April 5 chose a second site approximately six miles to the east.[69] This placed the new post, Fort Dodge, between the two fordable crossings of the Arkansas River in western Kansas. The Cimarron lay twenty-two miles west of the post, while a less suitable and less used fording area, the Mulberry Crossing, was situated approximately seventeen miles east of Fort Dodge.[70]

The initial fortifications raised at Fort Dodge were nothing more than crude earth dugouts excavated along the north bank of the Arkansas River. These dugouts were covered with brush and tents and then enclosed with a hastily thrown up earth barricade.[71] Modest though it was, Pearce had established the nucleus around which a permanent fort could later be constructed, but perhaps of greater importance in relation to Ford's immediate needs, he had erected a much needed base of operations for the anticipated campaign south of the Arkansas River. On April 9, mounts and saddles for the command arrived at Fort Larned,[72] and the following day Ford moved his troops toward Fort Dodge and the Cimarron.[73] Included in the twelve hundred men who rode with the general were several companies of "galvanized soldiers" or captured troops of the Confederacy who chose to campaign on the plains rather than remain in Union military prisons for the duration of the war.[74] The decision of Confederate prisoners to soldier in the Department of the Missouri was crucial to the summer campaign plans which had been drawn up by Dodge.

As the war drew to a close, Grant sent ten thousand federal troops to Fort Leavenworth for service on the plains; however, when news was received that the South had surrendered, the majority of these men were released from service on their protest that they had joined the army to fight the Confederacy and not Indians.[75] Of the seven thousand men finally assembled by Dodge for service with the department during the summer of 1865, five thousand were former Confederates.

Ford met only token resistence from the Indians on his march southward, with only a few minor skirmishes being fought before he reached the Arkansas River. As the general prepared to ford the river, he received a message from General Alexander McCook, a member of Leavenworth's hastily convened peace commission, ordering him to confine his military operations north of the river until the commissioners had parleyed with the Indians.[76]

As the talks between the commissioners and several chiefs of the Arapahoes, Apaches, Kiowas and Comanches continued through April, Ford was relieved of his duties and replaced by Brigadier General John B. Sanborn.[77] The new commander marched the unit back to Fort Larned in disgust. Dodge petitioned Grant to intercede with Secretary of War Stanton by asking that the military be permitted to proceed with the punishment of the hostiles who had so recently committed depredations along the frontier, but the pressure in Washington for arbitration of the Indian problem was too strong.[78]

By the middle of June several bands of Indians were again raiding wagon trains and settlements in western Kansas. As a result, Inspector-General D. B. Sackett was sent to the plains by the Secretary of War to view the Indian problem first hand, and he arrived at Fort Dodge immediately after a band of hostiles had driven off all the stock held by the post.[79] The raiding party had deceived the detail of herders assigned to guard the animals by riding slowly up to the herd dressed in blue army overcoats. They had then stampeded the animals with gunfire before the startled soldiers could react.

In his report General Sackett noted that a number of men had been killed and several hundred head of livestock stolen since General Sanborn's troops had returned to Fort Larned.[80] He suggested that a large cavalry force be sent into the field immediately to protect the commercial routes and settlements of western Kansas. The most serious attacks were being perpetrated by the Southern Cheyennes, who had refused to hold council with the peace commission.

Upon receipt of the Inspector-General's report Dodge ordered Sanborn to march southward again and to drive the Indians then raiding on the plains south of the Arkansas River.[81] While in the field south of Fort Larned, Sanborn received a communication from Leavenworth advising him that the chiefs of the Kiowas, Apaches, Arapahoes and Comanches were waiting to treat with him on Cow Creek.[82] On August 5, Sanborn agreed to suspend military action against these tribes if they would remain at peace until October 4, when a government commission would meet with them at the Little Arkansas River.[83]

The Treaty of the Little Arkansas

The most important provisions of the short-lived treaty of the Little Arkansas, which was agreed to on October 17, 1865, was the establishment of reservations for the tribes involved. The Cheyenne and Arapahoe holdings commenced south of the Arkansas River in Kansas, and extended southward into the Indian Territory; while the reservation for the Kiowas and Comanches was divided between northwestern Texas and the western extremity of the Indian Territory.[84]

Because the hastily formulated treaty granted lands to the Kiowas and Comanches in the Texas Panhandle which were not open for reservation assignment and at the same time placed the Cheyennes and Arapahoes on land previously allotted to the Cherokees, the tribes were left without a suitable home. All of the tribes involved in the treaty were for the time being given permission to hunt between the Platte and Arkansas Rivers during the summer months, but the reservation assignments were not unsnarled until 1869.[85]

This treaty proved to be of negligible value in bringing peace to the plains during the coming year. There was considerable evidence that the tribes involved had not intended to deal in good faith. Several attacks were carried out by bands on their way to negotiate at the Little Arkansas. The most serious of these occurred near Fort Dodge, where a party of Kiowas attacked a Mexican wagon train and killed five of the men.[86]

The Duplicity of Policy on the Indian Problem

From 1861 through 1865, no consistent government policy emerged to cope with the growing problem of the Plains Indians. When attacks became so numerous that they could no longer be tolerated, Kansas militia units were quickly formed and sent into the field. If the assaults reached epidemic proportions, as they had in 1864 and 1865, the army responded with punitive campaigns; but the military accomplishments of these thrusts were so insignificant that the Indian attacks continued unabated.

As the season for campaigning drew to a close in 1865, Grant was faced with increasingly heated protests from his officers in the field. They considered the army's opportunity to punish the Indians justly for their crimes along the frontiers had been needlessly frustrated by Secretary of War Stanton's refusal to allow them to carry the war south of the Arkansas River into the Indian Territory.[87]

Dodge's criticism of the ambiguity faced by the military is perhaps representative of the position taken by his fellow officers. In later years, after he had retired from the military service, the general noted:

> The policy of the United States in dealing with the Indian problem is beyond the comprehension of any sensible man. They were treated the same as foreign nations; and while they made treaties they never carried out their part of them, breaking them whenever the trend of civilization westward interfered with them in any way. The Government attempted to deal with and govern the Indians with civil agents and at the same time tried to enforce peace through the military authorities. This caused friction; and deception and cheating in the supplying of them through their contractors and civil agents brought untold complaints. If the Government had treated the Indians as a ward that they were bound to protect, as the English did, they would have had very little trouble in handling them. The military force would have held all conferences with them; fed them when they needed it; located them in an early day on unoccupied good hunting-grounds; and finally, as civilization moved into their territories and as their tribes wasted away, would have given them reservations where the Government from the money they received from the lands the Indians claimed, could have kept and fed them without any great burden or cost. In all the days of Indian warfare and treaties, there never was such a farce, or failure to comprehend the frontier situation, as in the years 1865 and 1866, and the failure of the Government to take advantage of the comprehensive plans instituted by the military authorities, as well as of the great expenditures made, and to punish the Indians as they deserved, brought, in after years, greater expenditures and more disturbances than ever.[88]

The memory of the Chivington Massacre and continued reports of bloodshed from the growing plains conflict led to increasing sharp criticism of the army's handling of the Indian problem by Congress and a number of Eastern newspapers. In the face of growing opposition to militarily crushing the Plains Indians, Grant sought to strengthen the position of the army on the Kansas frontier. While the Treaty of the Little Arkansas was being hammered out, the general ordered the establishment of two new military posts to protect the overland routes and settlements of western Kansas. This action indicates that Grant was not satisfied that this treaty, or perhaps any treaty, would bring peace to the plains.

On October 18, 1865, a post which eventually became Fort Hays was ordered established approximately sixty miles north of Fort Larned on the Smoky Hill Route.[89] This post was assigned the dual tasks of protecting the frontier and the Union Pacific Eastern Division railroad, whose surveying crews had been subjected to increased Indian harassment during the summer of 1865.

Another post, which became Fort Wallace, was ordered established on October 26, 1865, approximately one hundred and twenty-five miles west of Fort Hays, near the south fork of the Smoky Hill River. The line of major forts along the Smoky Hill and Santa Fe Routes had been completed.[90]

As part of Grant's plan for the future protection of the plains, the majority of the remaining disgruntled Union volunteers stationed in Kansas were released and replaced with four thousand Negro troops.[91] This rotation of men was thought necessary because of the mediocre performance of many of the volunteers in the field during the summer of 1865. It was also anticipated that Negro troops bore less prejudice against Indians.

During 1866 the United States Ninth and Tenth Cavalries were formed from the Negro troops.[92] Both units served with distinction in Kansas and the Indian Territory on several tours of duty extending from 1866 until 1872. These "buffalo soldiers," as the Indians often referred to them, in view of their dark kinky hair, had whites for field grade officers; however a few Negroes were commissioned as junior grade officers during their tenure on the plains.

The cessation of hostilities along the Kansas frontier in the fall of 1865 was to be expected with the approach of winter, and it in no way reflected any alteration of the Indians' plan to drive the whites from the buffalo hunting grounds between the Arkansas and Platte Rivers. They were, as yet, convinced that the inroads they had made during the Civil War years could be continued and that the settler's frontier could be steadily rolled back into eastern Kansas. When spring came again and green grass sprouted to feed their ponies, they would return once more to haunt the trade routes and settlements while challenging the army for supremacy on the plains.

CHAPTER II

FORT DODGE, 1865-1867: THE FORMATIVE YEARS

Dugout Soldiering

The troops who garrisoned Fort Dodge during the initial years of the post's existence undoubtedly questioned the wisdom of Captain Pearce's selection of a building site. The post rested on the north bank of the Arkansas River on a narrow meadow approximately one-fourth of a mile wide. The fort was overlooked by a limestone bluff to the north that rose from seventy to eighty feet above the elevation of the post. To the north of this bluff a series of prairie ravines blended into the open plains.

A factor of major consideration in selecting the site was the availability of water. Under sustained attack it would be necessary to have continual access to water, therefore the dugouts were placed as close to the river bed as possible. By choosing to build on the narrow meadow, the military surrendered the option of commanding the high ground which circled the post, except on the southern or river side. This plateau was later utilized by Indians to attack the post before preparations to receive the assault could be made by the men garrisoning the fort.[1] The shallow ravines to the north of the bluff were equally helpful to the Indians. Through the beds of these ravines they could easily approach the plateau without being detected by the soldiers below.[2]

There was little choice in the selection of building material for the post. The order to establish the fort required an immediate response by General Ford; yet the closest depot of supply, Fort Leavenworth, could not provide even the bare essentials for building, such as tools, nails and windows, for several months.[3] Unlike many rivers, the Arkansas offered almost no timber of construction quality. The military labor details engaged in the building process were forced to use the only abundant material available: the buffalo grass sod of the prairie.

During the course of the first year, seventy sod dugouts were completed.[4] The dimensions of each unit was ten by twelve feet in circumference, while the soddies were seven feet deep. The bottom five feet of depth was underground, and the dwellings were topped by a two foot ledge of sod that was then covered with cottonwood branches, brush and tents. The tents were of questionable value as the gusty prairie winds quickly tore them from their moorings.[5] A shallow door was fashioned along the south side of each dugout, facing the river, and a hole was left in the roof to provide fresh air and light. Each dugout was equipped with a sod chimney for heating and cooking during inclement weather.

Banks of earth were left around the inside perimeter of the dugout to be utilized as sleeping bunks. From two to four men were quartered in each unit.[6]

The location of the post and the crudeness of the dugouts left much to be desired in the fort's sanitation practices. During the spring the river usually flooded and underflow would invariably seep into the dugouts even if they were not actually submerged in flood water.[7] The ground on which the fort was situated was a mixture of silt and sand, and remained wet for some time following rains as a result of drainage from the high ground surrounding the post. Malarial fever, diarrhea, dysentery and pneumonia were usually frequent at Fort Dodge as a result of unsanitary quarters and exposure to the elements.[8] The monotonous diet of staples with a marked absence of fresh fruit or vegetables resulted in a prevalence of scurvy among the men of the garrison. The primary sanitation advantage of the closeness of the river was its service as a garbage dump and place of bathing for gritty soldiers willing to chance the treachery of the water's shifting sand and undertow.[9]

Mother nature compounded the woes of the garrison during the first winter at Fort Dodge. The blizzards of 1865 were unusually severe, and the troops were forced to shiver through the monotonous months with barely enough kindling to ward off the cold and cook their diet of plain food.[10] During much of the winter the fort was completely isolated from her sister posts as travel along the Santa Fe Trail ceased until spring had returned. While reminiscing on the post's first year of service, several years after he had retired from the army, General Dodge suggested that the post had been named for him by disgruntled soldiers who thought him personally to blame for their discomfort while stationed at such a primitive garrison.[11]

During the summer of 1866, the first shipments of lumber arrived from military depots in eastern Kansas. The nearest plentiful source of timber was approximately twelve miles from the fort; and because these groves were also of inferior quality, they could only be utilized for making corral fences and fire wood.[12] Officers' quarters and a temporary hospital were erected from sod and roofed with earth. The roofs of the dugouts were elevated, and wooden bunks were constructed from the lumber provided by the first supply train.[13] In an effort to ward off the elements condemned tents were used to line the roofs of the dwellings.

The heavy seasonal rains of late spring and summer quickly weakened all of the sod buildings, thereby appreciably dampening the enthusiasm of the garrison for continuing construction with that material. The sod found near the post was of poor quality, and continual soaking led to sagging walls and caved in roofs.[14] As the first civilian employees arrived to join the soldiers in erecting new structures, their labors were directed to the construction of badly needed storehouses and a corral for fifty horses.[15] A good portion of the quartermaster supplies were lost the first year through exposure to the elements.

In May, Fort Leavenworth offered to forward a portable saw to the garrison, however, the commanding officer asked that a field oven be sent instead. The saw would be of value only in cutting firewood and fencing, while the troops were complaining bitterly of being forced to eat bread which was heavily imbued with dirt and ashes while being baked in an earthen oven fashioned in the river bank.[16]

The almost total lack of diversion experienced by the garrison during the winter of 1865 was not easily forgotten; and they banded together the following spring as a volunteer labor force during their spare time to build a sutler's store, which their commander referred to as a "small miserable sod building."[17] By early summer a sutler, William Ladd, had been appointed; but his welcome by the troops was short lived. The merchandise sold by Ladd was supplied by his partner, Theodore Weichselbaum, who had secured a contract to operate several stores on military posts west of Fort Leavenworth.[18] In August the young commander of Fort Dodge, Captain Andrew Sheridan, reprimanded Ladd for charging the soldiers excessively for purchases made and ordered him to reduce his prices.[19] A Post Council of Administration was organized to oversee the sutler's store and any other civilian enterprises that might be undertaken near the fort in the immediate future.[20]

One of the most pressing needs of the young post was transportation. Permanent buildings required stone, and the nearest sites for quarrying lay from five to twelve miles to the north.[21] Wagons were also needed to haul timber from groves near the quarrying area. To alleviate this shortage, the post commander commandeered several wagons from government trains passing the post on their way to the Cimarron, and the strenuous task of quarrying and hauling began.[22]

During the fall and early winter of 1866, the difficulties of the command multiplied rapidly. Desertion became more attractive to the troops, who were faced with duty at the quarry or the lumbering site while on garrison duty, or the equally demanding rigors of long rides and Indian danger during field assignments.[23] Fall was a favored season for desertion as the troops realized that another winter of isolation and monotony was approaching. A small frame guardhouse was erected to confine wayward soldiers and civilians, but justice was meted out rather slowly. Several months often elapsed before the officers of the post could spare the time to convene court-martial hearings.

Occasionally lesser offenders were released without standing before a court-martial hearing because the length of their pre-trial confinement was considered a just disciplinary exaction for their crime.[24] The presence of growing numbers of civilian craftsmen and laborers eroded military discipline. The filthy condition of civilian dugouts so irritated the post commander that he ordered their quarters purged with disinfectant. He predicted that an epidemic of disease would be visited on the entire post if they did not become more sanitary in their living habits.

The public trains which frequently passed by the fort proved to be a serious problem for the garrison's officers. Enterprising wagon hands were well aware of the lucrative market for whiskey that could be found among the troops and civilians on the post, and gallons of the forbidden spirits were smuggled onto the post in spite of the rigorous inspections that were carried out by the post's officers.[26] Passing trains were favorite vehicles of escape for deserting troops, and it became necessary to send out mounted military details periodically to search the wagons of the prairie fleets for wayward soldiers from Fort Dodge or her sister posts along the Santa Fe and Smoky Hill Routes.[27]

The loss of personnel resulting from field engagements with the Indians and terminal sickness necessitated the establishment of a post cemetery. During 1865, seven troopers were buried at Fort Dodge, as well as a number of civilians who had either died while working at the post or had been killed near the fort during Indian raids.[28]

When orders were received in the spring of 1866 to establish a military reservation around the fort, survey parties were sent out to ascertain the location of the most advantageous terrain that might be included. It was decided that it would be necessary to establish the northern boundary of the reservation approximately fourteen miles above the post in order that adequate reserves of stone, timber and grass could be held for the future use of the garrison.[29] The western boundary commenced at the one hundredth meridian and extended in excess of five miles eastward at the widest point. Slightly more than forty-three thousand acres were included in the reservation.[30]

Post Service to the Frontier

Public citizens who stood accused of the commission of a felony while they were members of passing trains or in residence as employees of the post usually found themselves in the Fort Dodge guard house prior to being transferred to eastern Kansas for trial.[31] In addition to the service of confining frontier lawbreakers, the post distributed rations to destitute civilians. The bulk of these handouts were given to parties whose property had been lost during the course of an Indian attack or to drifting traders and trappers who were "down on their luck." The fare offered usually reflected the supplies presently held by the post and often included nothing more palatable than beans, coffee, flour and sugar.[32]

Many of the first ranches that were established in the vicinity of the post during the formative years proved to be frequent sources of trouble for the garrison. These enterprises were referred to as "whiskey ranches" by the military, thereby reflecting the intentions of their proprietors.[33] The Indian tribes along the Arkansas tolerated these "ranches" because they served as a primary source of liquor, guns and ammunition. An astute owner of such an undertaking could expect as much as twenty to one return on his investments when his trade goods were exchanged for horses, buffalo robes or annuity currency that had been given out to the Indians by government reservation agents.[34]

The officers at Fort Dodge considered the Bureau of Indian Affairs to be directly at fault for the sale of contraband whiskey and arms on the plains. The command complained bitterly to General Hancock, commander of the Department of the Missouri after the transfer of General Dodge in January, 1866, that Indians frequently arrived at the fort to collect their annuities armed with newly purchased revolvers.[35] Some of the more prosperous tribesmen had obtained several revolvers, which they valued over rifles because of their ease of handling while on horseback.

General William T. Sherman, commander of the Military Division of the Missouri, advised General Grant to confine the troops along the Santa Fe Route to their posts if the distribution of firearms was not stopped.[36] The general was persuaded that the soldiers along the frontier should not be expected to risk their lives to subdue the Indians if at the same time they were forced to engage an adversary that was armed — often better than themselves — by renegade ranchers and traders situated on the plains.

The greater issue of priority of authority in administering Indian affairs continued to smolder beneath the contest over the sale of contraband weapons to Indians.[37] Secretary of War Stanton was steadily pressed by the majority of his staff officers to have Indian relations transferred to the War Department, while the government Indian agents assigned to the plains tribes remained equally insistent that jurisdiction remain in the hands of the Department of the Interior.[38]

Building a Permanent Post

Throughout the years 1866 and 1867, the garrison labored to raise permanent facilities at Fort Dodge while keeping a watchful eye on the surrounding tribes of Plains Indians. Four companies of troops, two each of cavalry and infantry, divided their attention between frequent scouts and marches along the Santa Fe Route and work details which were organized from available troops to supplement the limited numbers of civilian workmen who had been hired for construction purposes. Because of the inadequacy of the old dugouts, two companies of troops were required to live in tents until permanent housing could be completed.[39]

Primary attention was given to the construction of two barracks, a hospital, a quartermaster building, a subsistence supply building and a headquarters building to house the commanding officer.[40] All of these structures were built of limestone that was laboriously quarried by both civilians and soldiers. Sixty teamsters and more than two hundred mules were kept busy hauling the heavy stones from the quarry to the construction sites.[41]

Lieutenant George A. Hesselberger guided the construction and demonstrated a taste for both durability and subtle beauty.[42] The stones used in building were of varying lengths; however, they were cut to eighteen inch heights and two foot thicknesses. The heavy stones were then dressed prior to their emplacement by civilian masons.

Each barracks building was designed to hold a company of approximately fifty men and was equipped with a kitchen and mess room in addition to a dormitory for the men.[43] The latrines were erected just behind the barracks. The hospital included a ward room adequate to house the anticipated sick of four companies, with an attached administration section for hospital personnel and a separate kitchen.[44]

The commanding officer's quarters was the only two-story structure built. The bottom floor included both living quarters and administrative rooms where the commanding officer could host his fellow officers for staff meetings or court-martial proceedings, while the second floor was reserved entirely for the commander's family.[45] Because of the elevation of the second floor and the field of fire thus provided, rifle ports were built at floor level to be utilized in case of sustained seige by hostile Indians.

In addition to the permanent stone buildings, several frame structures were added to fill the garrison's immediate needs until they could be replaced by more durable facilities. A blacksmith and carpenter shop was erected to house the craftsmen involved in the construction of new facilities.[46] When the blacksmiths were not engaged in their regular duties of providing hardware for building purposes, they were required to shoe several hundred head of horses and mules and to keep approximately sixty wagons in good repair. A temporary grain shed was created by extending a roof between the newly erected stone quartermaster and supply buildings.[47] The sod corral erected during 1866 was assigned to the quartermaster, and a second larger corral, roughly two hundred by one hundred fifty feet, was constructed in 1867 for the cavalry.[48] The exterior sides of both corrals were fashioned from sod. Their walls were approximately four feet thick and eight feet tall.

A small bake house was added to provide the cooking and baking facilities needed to feed the men living and working at the post. The two ovens of the bake house had a maximum capacity of five hundred rations of bread per day.[49]

Negro troops were segregated from the white troops and were quartered in a frame building which had neither plaster nor a ceiling below the roof.[50] Although Negro troop strength often grew to as much as two companies, only part of the forty by twenty foot structure was reserved for their use. The remainder of the building was utilized for storage. Segregation was also practiced by the hospital where a small five bed frame strucure was added to the main building to house Negro troops.[51] A parade ground approximately one hundred yards square was reserved at the center of the post by placing the permanent stone buildings around the perimeter and facing them inward.

During much of both 1866 and 1867, Lieutenant Hesselberger complained to the Department of the Missouri that construction progress was impeded by a shortage of both men and material.[52] Skilled craftsmen such as carpenters, masons and blacksmiths, who were willing to accept the difficult working conditions were paid from eighty-five to one hundred dollars per month, while common laborers were offered thirty-five dollars per month.[53]

The lumber and hardware needed to supplement the stone used in construction was brought in over the Santa Fe Trail by wagons from either eastern Kansas or Santa Fe, New Mexico. The latter was usually the favored source of supply, even though the materials had to be freighted a great deal further, because a much lower price was asked. In 1867, a thousand board feet of lumber could be delivered at Fort Dodge from Santa Fe for only thirty dollars.[54]

A good portion of the problems hampering construction at Fort Dodge were local in origin. During the fall of 1867, while strenuous efforts were being made to complete the buildings then under construction before cold weather suspended further work until the following spring, sporadic assaults were made by surrounding Indians on both the personnel and supplies of the post. Supply wagons headed for Fort Dodge were consistently attacked. One such raid netted the attackers a shipment of firearms and ammunition badly needed at the post as well as five wagons loaded with subsistence supplies.[55]

Similar raids were visited on work details sent out under military guard to quarry stone, cut firewood, procure lime for the post masons or to stack hay to be used by the fort's livestock during the winter months.[56] The size of these raiding parties varied from only a few to as many as several hundred participants. The impact of these attacks on post morale was critical. Few laborers cared to sweat on the plains of Kansas for only thirty-five dollars a month if the possibility of being murdered and scalped was included in the bargain.

During the last ten days of July, 1867, a cholera epidemic spread through the garrison, and twenty-one soldiers and civilians eventually died of the disease.[57] The illness was brought to Fort Dodge, as well as several other posts along the Santa Fe Trail, by a detachment of colored troops enroute to Fort Union, New Mexico, who had camped beside the fort for several days rest.[58] Major Henry Douglass, the commander of Fort Dodge, his wife and infant child contacted cholera; however, they all later recovered.

Except for the marauding of the "Lords of the Plains," the garrison could have anticipated the prospect of a reasonably comfortable winter in quarters; however, this luxury was not to be theirs. Ahead lay long rides, cold food, frostbite and occasional death as the contest for the plains continued without respite.

Fort Dodge and the Continuing Indian Problem

Throughout 1866 and 1867, a major portion of the western Kansas frontier was subjected to continued outbreaks of Indian hostility. The pattern of these attacks varied little from those committed during the late years of the Civil War. The commercial routes and the outer fringe of settlement were still favorite targets, but the newly established posts along the Smoky Hill and Santa Fe Routes bore an increasing share of the attacks as the natives sought to retain their supremacy on the plains.

Many of the attacks committed near Fort Dodge appear to have been unprovoked, while others were definitely precipitated by mistreatment of the Indians. In February, 1866, a party of freighters came to the post with a report that several Southern Cheyenne Indians had ridden into their camp six miles south of Fort Dodge; and after having been given tobacco and food by their hosts, they had killed and scalped a sixteen year old boy before the other members of the party could come to his defense.[59]

When the Cheyenne's agent, Major Edward W. Wyncoop, visited their camp two weeks later while distributing annuities, he inquired into the attack and was given a completely different account. The Cheyennes readily admitted killing the boy; however, they considered the act justified as the boy's father and several of his comrades had previously ridden into their camp and swindled a member of the tribe. The culprit, a Mr. Boggs, had persuaded one of the Cheyennes to trade eleven ten dollar bills for eleven one dollar bills. When the brave was later advised of the nature of the trade, he had ridden to the freighter's camp accompanied by several companions and demanded that the money be returned. On Bogg's refusal, a melee had ensued during which the boy lost his life.[60]

During the fall of 1866, scouts reported that several captive white women were being held by Indian bands encamped in the vicinity of Fort Dodge. In response to these reports, Lieutenant Hesselberger was ordered to take an interpreter and a guard of two enlisted men and investigate the rumors. Upon visiting a Kiowa camp some thirty-five miles below the fort, he discovered that the reports were true and was allowed to talk with two captive women. He learned that their names were Margaret and Josephine Box and that the teen-age girls had been captured, along with their mother and three other sisters, in August of the same year, while the Kiowas were raiding in northern Texas.[61] James Box, the father of the family, had been killed immediately while the others were taken as captives to a nearby Kiowa encampment. The youngest girl had died a few days after their capture, but the mother, Mary Box, and her daughters Maizie and Ida had been traded to a band of Apaches.

Lieutenant Hesselberger attempted to persuade the Kiowas that the girls should be turned over to his detail, but they refused to release the captives unless they were ransomed by the army.[62] On his return to Fort Dodge, the lieutenant reported the demands to the commanding officer, who authorized the purchase and delivery of the goods necessary to secure the release of the girls.[63] Word of the successful trade made by the Kiowas soon reached the band of Apaches holding the remainder of the Box women, and they immediately moved to an encampment close to the fort to negotiate for the ransoming of the captives they held.

Although a bargain on the terms of exchange was reached, General William T. Sherman visited Fort Dodge during an inspection tour and on hearing of the method used to secure the release of the first two girls, refused to allow the remainder of the family to be ransomed. Sherman reprimanded Sheridan for providing the demanded goods and ordered that no further exchange be made. The general feared that such a precedent would stimulate further attempts by plains tribes to capture white women and present them for ransom. Sherman then ordered that the proposed meeting for exchange proceed as planned. The leading tribesmen of the Apaches were then enticed into the fort to receive the ransom. Once there, they were placed under guard and threatened with death unless the remaining women were released.[64]

Artillery pieces were emplaced to command the approaches to the post, and every available soldier was stationed behind hastily erected barricades around the fort's perimeter. In the face of this show of determination, the captive Apaches signaled their waiting tribesmen to release the women and were in turn granted permission to rejoin their people.[65] Although General Sherman's reasons for refusing to pay ransom were perhaps sound, word of the apparent act of treachery spread to neighboring tribes; and relations between the Indians and the post deteriorated considerably in the wake of the incident.

As a direct result of the extension of the military frontier in Kansas along the Smoky Hill and Santa Fe Routes during 1864 and 1865, the transportation and settler's frontier moved rapidly westward into central Kansas during the following year. The incidence of depredations continued to grow as the Indians sought to prevent or delay the encroachment by the settlers and the railroads on their hunting grounds in western Kansas.

The terms of the Treaty of the Little Arkansas were suspended by both factions as the contest continued without interruption. The Department of the Missouri, vehemently supported by public sentiment within Kansas, considered the assault on the frontier to be ample evidence that a major campaign against the plains tribes was needed.[66] For their part, the Indians claimed that the treaty had been written under duress, that a number of the chiefs signing had been persuaded to do so while under the influence of alcohol, and that the annuities provision had not been upheld by the government.[67]

While the debate over the Indian problem continued in Washington, D. C., public pressure for military action continued to build in Kansas. During the summer of 1866, Governor Crawford yielded to the demands of his constituency and appointed General William Cloud to gather a battalion of militia to protect the frontier in lieu of the federal government's failure to do so.[68] Senators James Lane and Samuel Pomeroy of Kansas had guided the passage of a bill through Congress during the previous year that had given the Atchison and Topeka Railroads generous grants of right of way lands across the state.[69] Both the construction of the railroad and the profitable sale of railroad lands to settlers awaited a final settlement of the Indian problem. The militia unit attempted to patrol the Kansas frontier during both the summers of 1866 and 1867; however, the results of their marches were negligible. The first summer was spent along the settlements of central Kansas,[70] but in 1867 the battalion was moved to the western frontier to campaign in the vicinity of General Hancock's troops.

Perhaps a clue to the causes of the relatively mediocre performance of the troops was given by a correspondent traveling with them when he reported their response to the choice between fighting Indians or hunting buffalo:

> About the same time the Indians were seen, a herd of buffalo supposed to number at least five thousand were discovered in the distance, moving in the direction of our column. On came the vast herd at the top of their speed, presenting a grand, and, to the uninitiated, an awe-inspiring spectacle. As they approached the men became almost wild with excitement, and all efforts to restrain them were unavailing. The column wheeled spontaneously

into line and opened a brisk fire upon the advancing foe, which only served to change their course a little, when a general chase ensued; each man singled out his buffalo and pursued it until it bit the dust. More than a dozen were thus slain, and our hungry battalion enjoyed a rich feast of buffalo that evening.[71]

During the years 1866 and 1867, the focal point of the contest with the Indians was the area immediately surrounding Fort Dodge. The Cimarron continued to be a favored site of attack on the Santa Fe Trail, while the settler's frontier had by this time moved far enough west to be continually assaulted by bands of hostiles living close to the post.

In many ways the use of the Fort Dodge vicinity as a base of operations proved ideal for marauding Indians. A primary bone of contention between the Indians and the military was the delivery of adequate annuities.[72] The fort had become the primary site for distribution of annuities to several of the southern plains tribes.[73] Warring bands often left their women and children encamped near the post while they roamed the plains eastward in search of suitable prey.[74] As long as the women and children remained peaceful, they could expect the protection of the military. In fact, the presence of several government agents at Fort Dodge perhaps afforded them the greatest security there that they could expect to find anywhere on the plains.

Bids were taken annually from merchants competing for the right to supply goods through government contracts.[75] As headquarters for the Department of the Missouri, St. Louis had become the site for bid letting. In 1866, the bids for the blanket contracts varied from fifty-one thousand to one hundred seventy-one thousand dollars, while those for dry goods ranged from sixty-nine thousand to one hundred twelve thousand dollars.[76] The sharp competition between Eastern and Western merchants often led to the delivery of inferior goods to the Indians.

Unscrupulous traders usually offered the natives only two dollars and fifty cents for buffalo robes, which they wholesaled for eight dollars each.[77] Government agents claimed that their Indian wards were often forced to steal from neighboring tribes to feed their families. On the fringes of settlement there was an increasing incidence of Indian prostitution, as women sold themselves in exchange for food or clothing.[78]

The presence of several thousand disgruntled natives in the vicinity of Fort Dodge forced the garrison to consider the possibility that the post might be assaulted and taken if the Indians chose to do so.[79] Intelligence reports gathered at Fort Dodge indicated that the Sioux were attempting to persuade the Kiowa, Arapahoes, Cheyennes, Comanches and Apaches to commence a general war in western Kansas "as soon as the grass was one inch high." The Sioux promised to join in the struggle in force once the contest had been initiated by the southern tribes.[80]

Perhaps the most eloquent spokesman of the plains tribes was Satanta, a principal chief of the Kiowas.[81] He had distinguished himself as a native orator of unusual persuasion during several previous councils with the military, especially on the occasion of the signing of the Treaty of the Little Arkansas. His talent for verbal articulation so impressed his fellow chieftains that he was recognized as the primary arbitrator for the Arapahoes, Cheyennes and Comanches as well as the Kiowas.

During the winter of 1866, several councils were held between officers from Fort Dodge and Satanta through translation by an interpreter.[82] The chief berated both Agent J. H. Leavenworth and the government for their failure to provide promised annuities. He warned that a council would be held early the following spring between northern and southern tribes of the plains and that a general war was likely to follow.[83]

Satanta demanded that construction of new buildings at Fort Dodge cease and that the post, along with Fort Larned, be abandoned immediately. The chief noted that the soldiers were taking water, wood, buffalo and grass which belonged to him, and, as the government was not paying for these resources, he directed that no more be taken.[84] The wily Kiowa then asked that all military personnel be removed as far east as Council Grove, that the Santa Fe Trail be closed, and that construction of railroads and telegraph lines be immediately suspended on the plains of Kansas.[85]

He threatened to take the post the following spring as soon as the grass had grown to a sufficient height to support the ponies of his braves. Satanta added verbal salt to the wound created by his threats by noting that the horses and mules at Fort Dodge were rather gaunt and since the stock would be his as soon as he captured the fort, he suggested that proper attention be given to their feeding and care as he had no desire to own inferior animals.[86]

When the summary of the councils held at the fort was forwarded to the Department of the Missouri, orders were immediately returned directing the post to gather intelligence information as quickly as possible, relative to the intent of the southern tribes.[87] To carry out this task several additional guides and interpreters were engaged by the Fort Dodge command. Scouts were ordered to give particular attention to whether or not the women and children remained encamped near the fort. Their removal to a more remote encampment could be considered the prelude to an assault on the military posts or settlements of western Kansas.[88] The scouts were also directed to ascertain if guns and ammunition were still reaching the Indians through traders and to watch for the presence of Sioux Indians among the Southern tribes.[89] If Satanta's predictions were valid, council with the Sioux would precede a general assault by both the northern and southern plains tribes.

As a result of the ominous suggestions of coming violence on the plains, wagon trains wishing to move westward during the spring of 1867 were held at Fort Larned until a company of at least twenty could be assembled.[90] Each train was asked to elect a captain, and every adult male was required to have a suitable firearm for fighting Indians. In case of attack, the captain was expected to organize the defense of the train. Troop detachments were sent westward in relays with each group of wagons until the next post along the commercial routes was reached. Here the old guard was released, and a newly assigned detachment accompanied the train to the next post.[91]

By early March the contradictory and often confusing series of charges and explanations emanating from both the Bureau of Indian Affairs and the Department of the Missouri had been sufficiently reviewed by the Department of War. The olive branch of peace which was being offered by the government was apparently unacceptable to the plains tribes without the added promise that they would be allowed to retain the grazing grounds used by the buffalo herds on their annual migration through western Kansas. By late March the prairies were slowly greening in response to the added warmth of early spring, and the time had arrived for Satanta's predicted struggle for the plains.

Fort Dodge and the Hancock Campaign of 1867

On March 27, 1867, General Winfield S. Hancock moved his command westward from Fort Riley, Kansas. The primary task of the expedition had been outlined in the General Field Orders issued to the general explaining his mission on the plains:

> It is uncertain whether war will be the result of the expedition or not; it will depend upon the temper and behaviour of the Indians with whom we may come in contact. We go prepared for war, and will make it if a proper occasion presents. We shall have war if the Indians are not well disposed towards us. If they are for peace, and no sufficient ground is presented for chastisement, we are restricted from punishing them for past grievances which are recorded against them; these matters have been left to the Indian Department for adjustment. No insolence will be tolerated from any bands of Indians whom we may encounter. We wish to show them that the Government is ready and able to punish them if they are hostile, although it may not be disposed to invite war.[92]

On his arrival at Fort Larned, General Hancock's contingent was complemented by the addition of the U. S. Seventh Cavalry, commanded by General George A. Custer.[93] Shortly before the start of the march from Fort Riley, Agents Wyncoop and Leavenworth were advised to gather the primary chiefs of the plains tribes at Fort Larned for council with General Hancock.[94] Because of the wide dispersement of the tribes, north and south of the Arkansas River, it was difficult to assemble the chiefs on such short notice. General Hancock was openly critical of the tribes when he found that a number of their chiefs were missing when the initial council was convened. The general chose to consider their absence evidence of willful arrogance rather than the result of tardy notification.[95]

In addition to the field grade officers of Hancock's command and the group of Plains chieftains, a curious group of newspaper correspondents and area notables, such as David Butterfield of the Butterfield Stage Company, gathered to witness the proceedings. Perhaps the most illustrious member of the correspondents was Henry M. Stanley, who was collecting material for a book on frontier life, while earning a livelihood as a reporter. Young Stanley was destined to gain considerable fame in later years after he forsook the American West for Africa and succeeded in tracking down the elusive Dr. Livingstone.[96]

The general was noticeably blunt in declaring the objectives of the expedition:

> The Great Father has heard that some Indians have taken white men and women captives. He has heard, also that a great many Indians are trying to get up war. That is the reason that I came down here. I intend not only to visit you here, but my troops will remain among you, to see that the peace of the plains is preserved. I am going also to visit you in your camps. The innocent, and those who are truly our friends, we shall treat as brothers. If we find hereafter that any of you have lied to us, we will strike you. In case of war, we shall punish whoever befriends our enemies. If there are any tribes among you who have captives, white or black, you must give them up, safe and unharmed. I have collected all the evidence of all outrages committed by you, so that our agents may examine into the matter and tell me who are guilty, and who are innocent. When your agent informs me who the guilty are I will punish them; when just demands are made I will enforce them, if they be not attended to. I have heard that a great many Indians want to fight; very well, we are here, and are come prepared for war. If you are for peace, you know the conditions; if you are for war, look out for the consequences.[97]

General Hancock's statement of his intention to "visit" several of the tribes at their separate villages with his command immediately alarmed the Plains Indians.[98] The memory of Sand Creek lingered to remind them of another "visit," and as the campaigners moved southwestward toward Fort Dodge in mid-April, the bands encamped in their path melted away into the surrounding prairie.

As the expedition reached the Pawnee Fork of the Arkansas River below Fort Larned, scouts reported the presence of a large band of Cheyennes nearby under Chief Roman Nose.[99] When Hancock approached to within a few miles of the village, Roman Nose and three hundred of his braves appeared in battle formation on a hill directly in the line of march. A brief parley was held; however, the general refused their offer to council outside the encampment so that the women and children would not be frightened by the presence of his soldiers, and the troops then continued the march toward the village. Custer was sent ahead with the Seventh Cavalry to surround the Indians.[100] When he had advanced to within sight of the encampment, returning scouts advised him that the Cheyennes had fled from their homes prior to Custer's arrival and that they apparently were moving northward toward the Smoky Hill Route.

Hancock considered this act of disobedience intolerable and ordered Custer to pursue the Cheyennes while he proceeded to gather the abandoned belongings of the band and put them to the torch. Newspaper correspondents present considered the material value of the village to be at least one hundred thousand dollars.[101] Huge piles of buffalo robes, which would bring as much as twenty dollars each on the Eastern market, were destroyed along with considerable quantities of household goods which the Cheyennes had been forced to leave behind by the suddenness of their departure. The list of these goods, which were recorded by several of the correspondents prior to their destruction, offers an excellent opportunity to examine the changes effected on Indian customs by their increased consumption of American leather goods, hardware and household articles. Several hundred horned saddles, axes, frying pans, lariat ropes, chairs, sacks of paints and doormats were destroyed, as well as lesser quantities of hammers, crowbars, coffee pots, pitchforks, scythes, ovens and coffee mills.

General Hancock later attempted to justify the burning of the Cheyenne village on the grounds that he had received word from Custer that two men had been killed along the Smoky Hill Route as a result of Indian depredations; however, no positive identfication of the tribal affiliation of the guilty was ever made.[102] The general was apparently satisfied that all tribes should collectively bear guilt for such acts if the alternative was that none should be punished.

After chastising the Cheyennes, the command continued the march to Fort Dodge. Military couriers were sent to all the posts along the Santa Fe and Smoky Hill Routes advising them of the flight of the Cheyennes as well as recommending that they prepare for a fresh assault on the frontier.[103] The garrison at Fort Dodge was ordered to patrol the Cimarron and either to take the hostiles they encountered into custody or to engage them on the field.[104] By this action Hancock hoped to block the Indian exodus from his path of march. The general was well aware of the continuing friction between the military and the Plains tribes in the vicinity of that post, and he hoped to review the situation first hand. Major Douglass turned out the entire garrison and fired a fifteen gun salute in honor of the general's arrival.[105] The correspondents moving with the expedition were quite favorably impressed with the strenuous efforts which were being made by the garrison to build permanent facilities to replace the old sod quarters, but they questioned the wisdom of making "quarrymen, common laborers and clodhoppers" out of men who had enlisted in the army to guard the frontier.[106]

At Fort Dodge, Hancock learned that a sharp engagement had just been fought near the Cimarron between a detachment of cavalrymen from the fort and a band of Sioux and Cheyenne warriors. Six braves had been killed and one cavalryman had been shot through the thigh during the running exchange of gunfire over five miles of prairie.[107] This contest produced the first bloodshed directly related to the Hancock campaign.

The general was again disappointed as he had earlier been at Fort Larned, by the absence of several Indian chieftains with whom he had hoped to hold council. News of the burning of the Cheyenne village had preceded the general to the fort, and Satanta and Satank's bands of Kiowas as well as Little Raven's Arapahoes had vanished into the prairie to the south before the

Cimarron could be closed. Only Kicking Bird's encampment of Kiowas remained to parley with the army.[108] After advising Kicking Bird to keep his people south of the Arkansas River so that they might not be mistaken as a hostile band and punished by the army along with those remaining north of the river, the general offered to hire several braves as scouts for the military posts in the area, and then ordered his command to prepare to march back to Fort Larned.

On the return of the expedition to that post it was found that several chieftains, including Satanta, had notified their agents that they were willing to council with General Hancock. When the chiefs had been assembled, the general once again repeated the motives of his campaign before the grievances of the Indians were heard.[109] Satanta was selected by the chieftains to be their spokesman, and the Plains orator treated the post to an unusual display of verbal cunning.[110] After criticising the Kiowa agent, Colonel Leavenworth, for failing to deliver promised annuities, the wily chief noted that although the military had cut down his trees, used his grass, killed his buffalo, he remained a true friend. Satanta declared that the Kiowas had refrained from taking to the warpath largely because of his personal intervention, and he promised that his people would continue to maintain peaceful relations along the frontier after the withdrawal of Hancock's expeditionary force from the plains.[111]

As he reached the climax of his oration, Satanta pledged his willingness to go to war at the side of the army to eliminate hostilities on the plains even if this meant fighting against his fellow Indians. His apparent display of good faith so impressed Hancock that he offered to hire three hundred of Satanta's braves as scouts for the Department of the Missouri. The general then gave the Kiowa chief a brigadier general's full dress coat, complete with epaulettes and sash, and a plumed officer's hat as a token of his personal pleasure with the promises made by the chief.[112]

While Hancock lectured and listened at Fort Larned, Custer moved the Seventh Cavalry along the Smoky Hill Route in search of hostile Indians. The frustration of repeatedly pushing his command to the site of a recent raid only to find that the Indians had vanished so irritated the general that he seemed to redouble his efforts on each such occasion to engage his elusive adversary before they could commit acts of violence at some other point.[113]

The campaign of 1867 was perhaps the most trying military experience of Custer's career prior to his engagement with the Sioux at the Little Big Horn. The saddle weary troops of the Seventh Cavalry deserted in droves along his line of march. More than eight hundred deserted during this single season of campaigning.[114]

When cholera epidemics broke out in several of the military posts of western Kansas, the general deserted his command in the field between Fort Wallace and Fort Hays and quickly returned to Fort Riley where he had left his wife before the start of the spring campaign. His later plea before a court-martial, that he was after supplies for his troops, was not accepted and he was suspended from command for one year. More likely he suspected his wife might fall victim to cholera.[115]

Hancock and Custer's inability to find hostile Indians was not shared by the garrison at Fort Dodge. In fact, the command was hard pressed to meet the challenge being meted out along the Santa Fe Route. In the wake of the withdrawal of the primary campaign force, a rash of depredations and attacks was committed.

The opening assault was made at the Cimarron where Satanta's Kiowas attacked several trains and succeeded in overrunning a number of wagons including one caught during the process of fording the river.[116] Four men were killed during the attack, and a number of others were wounded. Several wagon loads of goods were taken, as well as ninety-eight head of cattle. In violation of the rules stipulated by the military for caravans traveling the route, none of the train's members were armed, and as a result no defense of the train was made. A second train owned by several Mexican merchants was attacked the next day south of the Arkansas River. Although there was no loss of life, a considerable amount of livestock was taken.[117]

The commander of Fort Dodge responded by sending every available cavalry trooper into the field in search of the marauders.[118] Although his action was consistent with the general military mission of the post, on this occasion it proved to be a grave error.

In the past Satanta had been a frequent visitor at Fort Dodge, and he was quite aware that the extensive scouts and marches being carried out in the field by the post's limited reservoir of troops had reduced the remaining garrison to a dangerous level. The Kiowa chieftain responded by dealing the fort the most embarrassing blow the young post had yet experienced. On the twelfth of June, he led approximately two hundred of his braves on a raid designed to capture as many of the fort's horses and mules as possible, thereby setting the garrison on foot, and neutralizing their effectiveness in the field.[119] The attack was timed to fall simultaneously on the quartermaster and cavalry herds while they were pasturing near the post. The quartermaster mules were saved when the Indians were discovered approaching the herd, and the guards had stampeded the animals back to the post before the raiders arrived. The detail with the cavalry horses was less fortunate. Satanta's attack came as a complete surprise, and the entire herd was lost.[120] One of the four guards assigned to the horses was fatally wounded during the raid. As the captured herd was driven past the garrison, Satanta doffed his plumed officer's hat to the startled soldiers watching the raid from the safety of the post, and continued on his way.[121]

Ten horses which had remained at the post while the herd was pasturing were immediately saddled, and a small detachment was sent in pursuit. A second unit of several wagons of infantry pulled by quartermaster mules followed, but the bulk of the herd was never recovered. When the small mounted unit neared a creek west of the post, they came upon Satanta attempting to catch six straggling horses. They succeeded in killing his mount, but the crafty

Kiowa chief escaped without personal injury.[122]

While the Fort Dodge garrison was temporarily reduced to spectator status, Satanta initiated yet another series of assaults on the mail stations and wagon trains along the Santa Fe Route. Until a new herd of cavalry horses could be secured, the post was to remain relatively ineffective. The detachment at each mail station between the western post was increased from four to eleven men.[123] Earth walls were thrown up around the stations to ward off attacks. However, several of the stations were raided with considerable loss of life to both military and civilian personnel stationed there.

Major Douglass reported to the Department of the Missouri that:

> The country in this vicinity is alive with Indians who operate in bands numbering from fifty to two hundred. By the loss of the cavalry herd I am sadly crippled. One company is hardly sufficient to operate with advantage. The Indians have many war parties out in different directions and while pressing them in one direction, they commit depredations in another. There is no doubt but that all the Indians of this country are at war with us. Their peace promises were only mere pretexts to gain time.[124]

A steadily lengthening casualty list testified to the repeated success of attacks carried out at the Cimarron. Eleven men were killed at that site during one such raid on a train which had again been struck while fording.[125] Station duty on the Smoky Hill Route was considered so hazardous that men refused to accept employment along the express road.[126] Women passengers were noticeably absent on the commercial trails from Ellsworth, Kansas, to Denver, Colorado.

The newspapers of Kansas heaped criticism on the army for its failure to reduce the Indian menace. The editor of the *Junction City Union* noted that:

> There does not appear to be enough soldiers to protect the Santa Fe Route, let alone hunt Indians. I can't tell what the devil the government means, men are being butchered every day and no attempt is made to bring the war to a close.[127]

The *Rocky Mountain News* of Cherry Creek, Colorado Territory tabulated that it was presently costing the government twenty-four thousand dollars to kill each Indian on the Kansas plains, and the editors offered to enlist a mercenary unit of Colorado militia to assist in the fighting on a contract basis. Twenty dollars was thought to be a sufficient bounty for each dead Indian if the militiamen were allowed to keep scalps and ears for later sale as souvenirs.[128] As the debate between the East and the West over the proper procedure for handling the Indian problem flared anew, a beleagured General Pope at departmental headquarters in St. Louis facetiously suggested that a large reservation should be established in the heart of the urban East so they might experience first hand the depredations of the noble Redman.[129]

Pope asked the commander of Fort Dodge to explain charges currently being levied by wagonmasters and newspapers in western Kansas that the garrison had willfully neglected to provide proper protection for Mexican trains near the Cimarron.[130] Major Douglass's reply that the command had diverted as much time and manpower as possible to the crossing was considered inadequate, and Inspector-General R. B. Marcy was dispatched to the fort to review the military situation along the Santa Fe Trail.

As the general neared Fort Dodge, he was given a first hand demonstration of the garrison's primary problem. Little Robe's band of Cheyennes attacked his train and killed an officer who was riding as a flanker, while critically wounding an enlisted man.[131] The ferocity of the assault left Marcy thoroughly shaken. Shortly after his arrival at the fort, word was received that a wagon train was under siege at the Cimarron, and the general, usurping Douglass's privilege of command, personally ordered a detachment of cavalry into the field to engage the attackers.[132]

Although he remained at Fort Dodge for only one day, the Inspector General forwarded a hasty but caustic analysis of the post's performance to the Department of the Missouri.[133] In his report he was generous in his criticism of the personal conduct of Douglass. Marcy asked that the fort's commander be censured for dereliction. In his opinion, too much money and manpower had been utilized for construction purposes while the frontier remained inadequately protected.[134]

When asked to comment on these charges by departmental headquarters, Douglass forwarded a bitter denial of their accuracy. He noted that the Inspector General had been "unduly excited" by the presence of Indians along the route of travel and that the three hundred attacking savages mentioned in Marcy's report were actually only sixty in number.[135] He stated that in light of the inexperience and insuffiicient size of his command, all that was humanly possible was being done to protect the area surrounding the post.

The captain's reply to the charges that excessive time and expense had been given to building quarters so magnificent and smoothly dressed that they "appeared to be designed for the National Capitol" was especially acidic. He considered the buildings to have been constructed as economically as possible under existing circumstances. The captain pointed out that the winters on the plains were unusually harsh and only first rate materials and construction procedure could provide the men of the garrison with decent barracks. Perhaps the suggestion that lavish quarters had been built at Fort Dodge was especially irritating to the captain in the light of the recent death of his wife. He bitterly attributed this loss to the woman's exposure to the elements while trying to make a home of a "small frame hovel."[136]

Although Major Douglass was later vindicated of any personal responsibility for the losses sustained by recent Indian attacks or of improper conduct relative to the erection of new buildings, the officer directly responsible for their construction, Lieutenant George A. Hesselberger, was called before a court-martial hearing at departmental headquarters and dismissed from the service for misuse of government funds.[137] The court-martialing of the lieutenant was not the result of his construction practices, rather of his inability to account for the disbursement of a portion of the money supposedly spent for materials and labor. In recognition of his personal disgrace, a buffalo robe was hung over the dedication stone of the newly completed buildings. The stone bore the imprint of Hesselberger's name.[138]

The Treaty of Medicine Lodge

As the fall of 1867 approached, new dimensions were being called for in the nation's Indian policy. If the Hancock Campaign had been disappointing to both the Department of War and the Bureau of Indian Affairs, the results of the abortive expedition, for quite opposite reasons, were even less palatable to settlers of western Kansas and the Eastern advocates of fair play in dealing with the Indian.[139] A good portion of the national public had long since wearied of the apparently unending bloodshed that gripped the plains annually from early spring until late fall.

Prior to the campaign of 1867, the people of Kansas had stood firmly behind the conduct of the army on the plains, even during the exacting Civil War years when the absence of adequate military protection had been sorely felt. However, their patience had worn thin during the season just past when neither Hancock nor the sentinel military posts along the frontier had proved capable of coping with the growing Indian menace.[140]

Curiously enough, the Indian Commission had little difficulty in reaching warring bands for purposes of council, even while they were raiding on the plains. During the difficult months of August and September when the Fort Dodge garrison had detachments constantly in the field engaging war parties, preliminary peace talks were being held at the fort with several chiefs of the belligerent tribes prior to the general council that was later called at Medicine Lodge Creek.[141]

When word of these talk reached the general public the military in general, and the Fort Dodge garrison in particular, were bitterly censured by the press. One irritated critic went so far as to suggest collaboration on the part of the officers of Fort Dodge:

> The latest news from the Indian Peace Commissioners is exeedingly flattering — to the Indians.
>
> On the 5th or 6th of this month, Satanta, the chief of the Kiowas, went to Fort Dodge, and by professions of peaceful intentions procured from the soft-headed military authorities arms and ammunition to hunt with. As soon as these nice little things were in their possession, the red-skins, numbering about one hundred, went out on the rampage.
>
> These military officers on the plains are getting to be very interesting institutions and if they keep on will be able to succeed Andy Johnson. We have yet to hear of over two cases where the regular officers or soldiers have been of any use in fighting the red-skins. They appear to take delight in witnessing the murders by Indians, and the plundering of trains, without offering any help to the white men.[142]

Above the caustic barbs of the western frontier, and undoubtedly of greater concern to a constituency-conscious Congress, the Eastern plea for a final, but more humane, settlement of the Indian dilemma continued to grow ever more demanding. Congress responded to the latent awakening of the national conscience by appointing an unusually illustrious Peace Commission to treat with the Indians, which included Commissioner of Indian Affairs Nathaniel G. Taylor, Senator John B. Henderson, Generals William T. Sherman, William S. Harney, Alfred H. Terry and Christopher C. Augur and Colonel Samuel F. Tappan.[143] The members were instructed that permanent peace, with justice, was to be made with the plains tribes.

When the council opened at Medicine Lodge on October 2, 1867, Governor Crawford of Kansas was present as a result of a personal invitation from General Sherman to witness the proceedings. The Governor had spent much of the past summer at Topeka ordering units of Kansas Militia to different sections of the state in response to irate demands from the citizenry that he provide increased protection along the frontier. Governor Crawford noted with a jaundiced eye that:

> The Indians were there in force; bucks, squaws and papooses, five thousand or more, besides their ponies, dogs and stolen horses and mules. A train of supplies was brought down to the council grounds and the boxes of goods piled up on top of each other in full view, that the Indians might come in and take notice. No boxes were set apart or piled up for the white women and children whose husbands and fathers had been killed and scalped by the fiendish devils who were waiting for the goods in these boxes.[144]

Forty-eight chieftains representing the Kiowas, Comanches, Apaches, Southern Cheyennes and Arapahoes assembled with the commissioners in a large tent; and after the formalities of hand shaking and smoking the peace pipe were completed, the council got down to serious bargaining.[145] The gross naivete of a number of the chieftains became immediately apparent during the course of the negotiations. Several had no comprehension of the permanency of a treaty, being persuaded that these agreements were drawn up periodically as something of a ritual and that the land they had earlier given up had automatically reverted to them when once hostilities were again resumed.[146] Others were unaware that their tribes had even ceded land to the government. They still considered all the land west of the Mississippi River to belong to the plains tribes.[147]

A few of the more astute chiefs, such as Satanta of the Kiowas and Tall Bull of the Cheyennes, realized that the tribes were being asked to renounce permanently all claims to the hunting grounds between the Platte and Arkansas Rivers. After remaining silent during the early negotiations, they later advised their fellow chieftains to refuse to sign away their homes.[148]

There is considerable evidence that the representatives of neither side negotiated in good faith at Medicine Lodge; however, both were required to counsel because of their separate instructions and needs.[149] The Peace Commission had been ordered to formulate a treaty that would bring permanent peace; and regardless of their previous experience to the contrary, they pressed the Indians to sign the treaty, undoubtedly still convinced that spring would bring renewed war on the plains.

Although the Indian representatives held out stubbornly, it was perhaps necessary that they eventually relent and sign the document. Winter was approaching; and unless they agreed to the terms of the commission, annuities would be withheld and many of their kinsmen would undoubtedly starve before spring. The reluctance of many of the chiefs was overcome through the distribution of a large quantity of liquor.[150] The whiskey appeared, at least temporarily, to help them forget their unfortunate past experiences with the government at the bargaining table.

By the terms of the treaty the signatory tribes relinquished all claims to the plains between the Platte and Arkansas Rivers, including the privilege of seasonal hunting.[151] The Comanches, Kiowas and Apaches were given a reservation within the western Indian Territory between the Red and Washita Rivers, while the Cheyennes and Arapahoes were placed on a tract directly to the north, between the Red and Arkansas Rivers.[152] The commission also promised to provide seeds, farming implements and supervisors to help establish the tribes agriculturally.[153]

At the end of the Council, the huge pile of boxes was opened by the Indians. Blankets, food, clothing and surprisingly enough, a large quantity of guns, ammunitions and hunting knives were distributed to the tribes.[154]

When the terms of the Treaty of Medicine Lodge reached Fort Dodge, the garrison immediately recognized that the post had been given a difficult military mission for the future. A definite line had been established between the Indians and the settler's frontier across southern Kansas. For several years to come, whenever bands of malcontents decided to break out of their reservations and move northward via the Cimarron toward their old buffalo hunting grounds, orders would be sent to the post to "hold the line of the Arkansas."

Kansas State Soldiers Home
Fort Dodge

SOD HOUSE SOLDIERS' QUARTERS

General Pope described these sod dugout soldiers' quarters as "holes not fit to be dog kennels," yet they served the post adequately until permanent buildings could be raised.

CHAPTER III

SOLDIERING ON THE PLAINS

Garrisoning the Troops

For the most part, the barracks assigned to the enlisted men at Fort Dodge were of better quality than the quarters reserved for the garrison's officers. A third barracks, built of sod, was added shortly after the completion of the two stone barracks in 1867, thereby providing adequate accommodations for an additional company of troops.[1] With the exception of the commanding officer, who was comfortably quartered in one of the permanent stone structures, the officers of the post fared little better than married enlisted men. Both were garrisoned in rather crude sod or frame buildings.[2]

Single enlisted men were bunked in large dormitory rooms which were centrally located in all of the barracks buildings. Each dormitory contained two double tiers of bunks along the outside walls which would accommodate a total of forty-four soldiers.[3]. The barracks were heated with wood burning cast-iron stoves. Although a small supply of bituminous coal was freighted to the post to fuel the forges of the blacksmith's shop, the expense of hauling such a bulky item across the prairies forced the post to utilize wood for both cooking and heating purposes. Each man was given a kindling allotment which he was expected to use each month. Because the allowance was not cumulative, surpluses were periodically collected during the summer, and no increase in allotment was given for the winter months when cold weather necessitated burning more fuel.[5] Although the soldiers complained bitterly that their barracks were often cold during the winter, the wood rations remained the same for each month of the year. Drinking water was obtained from wells located behind each barracks, while water for all other uses was taken from tank wagons which were replenished daily from the nearby river.[6]

There were no indoor accommodations for washing, shaving or bathing. The troops were provided with a wooden trough behind each barracks for those purposes,[7] which could be filled from a nearby water barrel. The post surgeon, who was charged with regularly inspecting the troops' personal hygiene habits, chronically complained to the commanding officer and the Office of the Surgeon General at Washington, D. C., that the men of the garrison should bath more frequently.[8] This situation was alleviated somewhat during the warmer months when the river could be used for bathing; however, few soldiers could be persuaded to break the ice on the trough and wash during the grip of a Kansas winter.

The government's monetary consideration for the enlisted men was modest, but apparently sufficient to secure the necessities for soldiering with perhaps a few dollars left over each month for purchasing "the better things of life" from the post sutler's store. Privates were paid thirteen dollars per month during their first two years of service.[9] Increments for years of service or promotion increased the base pay so that a corporal usually drew from fifteen to twenty-dollars per month, while a first sergeant's pay ranged from twenty-five to thirty dollars.[10] A visiting paymaster, who served several posts within the same military department, paid the troops either monthly or bi-monthly, depending on his ability to get to the post.[11] When winter weather or summer Indian hostilities made travel hazardous, the troops relied on credit from the sutler to tide them over until the next pay call. The professional soldier could retire after twenty-five years of service and receive two-thirds pay for the remainder of life.

The clothing allotment provided by the government was usually sufficient; however, troops were required to pay for articles drawn in excess of the enlistment allowance.[12] A thrifty soldier who did not claim all of his clothing allotment was given a cash payment when he was mustered out from the army for those items not used.

Post laundresses, who provided their own soap and starch, washed the enlisted men's clothing for the fee of one dollar per dozen for large garments and fifty cents per dozen for smaller items.[13] Although the enlisted men were required to clean their own quarters, the officers had servants to perform this task as well as to launder their clothes and to prepare meals for them.[14]

Army Mess

Mess for the enlisted men was organized on an individual company basis. Each barracks contained a kitchen and subsistence storeroom for that purpose. Cooks were detailed monthly from among the men of each company on a rotation basis.[15] Consequently the quality of food served was closely correlated with the culinary talents of those thus selected. By "pulling strings" with the commanding officer, company sergeants occasionally left men of superior cooking skill on detail for several months or perhaps permanently, if the duty was acceptable to the men involved.

Food staples, such as flour, sugar, salt, coffee, bacon and salted meats were supplied periodically by government trains. As the westerly movement of the settler's frontier approached the post, a greater variety of food was made available and an officer was frequently detailed to nearby communities to purchase perishables such as potatoes, cabbage and onions for the use of the garrison.[16]

Each enlisted man was given a bread allowance of eighteen ounces per day.[17] During the early years of the post's existence the troop's meat rations consisted of salt pork and freshly killed buffalo, antelope or game birds hunted in the area immediately surrounding the post.[18] By 1870, ranches near the fort provided beef on a contract basis, and a steer was killed daily to feed the men.

Several attempts were made to cultivate a post garden as a source of dietary supplement; however, the marginal rainfall of western Kansas was usually not adequate to sustain plant growth during the heat of summer.[19] In addition to the problem of dry weather, the livestock of the post proved to be a constant menace to the garden when they broke out of corrals or escaped from the not always watchful care of the herders.

Although the food was plain and often poorly prepared, the garrison eagerly answered the call to mess. Soldiers who rushed to the table or displayed intolerably bad manners were sent away from the mess hall until such time as they could properly restrain themselves.[20]

The post surgeon periodically inspected the mess offered the troops and recommended changes in diet and kitchen sanitation practices.[21] His primary complaint to his superiors in Washington, D. C., was that fresh foodstuffs were seldom available and consequently scurvy remained a chronic medical problem of the fort. Left-over or spoiled food was gathered in a "slop wagon" and dumped in the nearby river.[22] Ice was taken from the river each winter and stored in a sod building under hay. Except during unusually hot summers or when several additional companies of men were bivouacked near the post, ice was available to the men until late summer.[23]

Work Details

In addition to the regular military duty that a soldier might expect during the time he remained on the post, the troops of Fort Dodge were assigned to work details at the stone quarry, the lime kiln, the hospital, the hay fields and the fort's timber tracts. The work crews usually consisted of from three to twelve men, and the length of assignment varied from one to three weeks.[24]

Because of the arduous nature of the labor required, men were often sent to these details as a result of disciplinary action. The quarry, kiln, hay fields and timber tracts were all some distance from the fort, thereby necessitating that the troops bivouac near the site of labor during their tour of duty. Both the officers and men of Fort Dodge complained that civilians should be hired for such duty, but the scarcity of available labor forced the assignment of soldiers to the details. By 1870, the problem of securing civilian labor had noticeably lessened. Nearby ranchers accepted government contracts to provide wood and hay for the post, while at the same time construction no longer required large assignments of men to either the quarry or the kiln.[25]

Men were placed on duty as hospital stewards on much the same rotation basis as were the company cooks. Occasionally men could be persuaded to accept permanent duty at the hospital; but for the most part, the task of caring for the sick and wounded was considered rather unmanly, and assistance for the post surgeon could be procured only through forced assignment.[26]

Post Education and Spiritual Life

During the spring of 1868, a frame building that had been hastily erected the previous summer to isolate cholera victims was converted to a recreation parlor.[27] This action brought an immediate protest from the post chaplain, Major A. G. White, who considered the educational and moral guidance due the troops of the garrison to have been neglected while a degrading amusement hall had been established.[28] As a result of his letter of criticism to department headquarters, Major Douglass was ordered to offer the building to the chaplain as a school during the daylight hours of the week from Monday through Friday, and as a church on Sunday morning. Although Major White continued to complain that a "gambling hall" was no place to conduct school activities or worship God and that he resented preaching from a billiard table rather than a pulpit, regular classes and church services were organized by the summer of 1868, and continued thereafter.[29]

According to military regulations, the post assumed the responsibility of providing elementary education for enlisted men as well as for the children of the garrison. The curriculum consisted of classes in reading, writing, arithmetic, geography and history.[30] Classes were dismissed for the children during the summer months when the heat of the poorly ventilated school room made studying difficult, and for the older students from among the enlisted men whenever their services were required on scouting details or campaigns.[31]

Garrison Military Routine

The soldier's day commenced early on the plains. Company trumpeters assembled at 4:30 A.M., and blew reveille at 5:00 A.M. Breakfast and stable calls were sounded immediately after reveille formation, and sick call followed at 6:30 A.M. Company areas were policed following fatigue call at 6:45 A.M. Drill call followed immediately after early morning fatigue duties were completed. The troops were recalled from drill at 8:15 and, except for those who were mounted as guards at 8:50, they remained on fatigue call until dinner call at 12:00 P.M.

After a one hour respite for dinner, the garrison returned to fatigue duty until 5:00 P.M. Between recall from afternoon fatigue and supper, which was usually served at 6:00 P.M., the troops fell out for afternoon stable call and water call. Tattoo was blown at 9:00 P.M., and the day's routine ended with taps at 9:30 P.M.[32]

Infantrymen spent several hours each week practicing close order drill and skirmishing,[33] while the cavalry troops gave one hour each day to grooming their horses, to practicing saddling and mounting, and to drilling while on horseback.[34]

Target practice was held monthly for both infantrymen and cavalrymen.[35] Prisoners from the guardhouse were allowed to participate in target practice; and when weather was bad, the entire garrison fired at makeshift indoor targets.[36] Scores were kept by measuring the inches from the center of the bulls eye for each of the ten shots fired, then totaling the measurements for a composite score.[37] The soldier with the least number of total inches each month was declared the "prizeman" and was relieved of guard duty for the following month and given a two day pass to spend as he chose.[38]

Equipment Trials

Before new weapons or equipment was adopted by the army, extensive field trials were usually held; and the Fort Dodge garrison was often called upon to participate in such tests. In 1870, competitive trials were held at the post between the Improved Springfield and Remington rifles, and the results, which reflected the troops' opinion of their relative merits, were then relayed to department headquarters.[39]

During the following year when the army was considering replacing the traditional bayonet with a dual purpose weapon called a "trowel bayonet," extensive field trials were carried out by the garrison. The trowel bayonet was so named because of its close resemblance to the standard mason's tool of that name. It was hoped that the bayonet could be used as an entrenching tool in addition to its usual service in close combat.

The officer in charge of the trials complained that the new bayonet bent badly when used for entrenching purposes and often injured the hands of those attempting to dig with it. He also noted that two sets of picks and shovels would move more dirt than thirty of the new bayonets. What concerned the officer most, however, was the shortness of the trowel bayonet. He noted that they were more than eight inches shorter than the older models, and he recommended that they not be adopted unless "your antagonists will agree to arm themselves with the same bayonet."[40]

Unfortunately for the men of the garrison, they were not always asked to try new equipment before it was adopted as standard army issue. Occasionally supposedly serviceable items were issued to the troops, who then promptly discarded them. Such was the case when a detachment of cavalry troops was given new cartridge belts and rifle slings just prior to its departure for an extended scout along the frontier. The new belts and slings were so heavy and inflexible that they chafed the soldiers to such an extent that they were thrown away in the field and temporarily replaced with the surcingle from their saddles.[41] One issue of campaign hats was found to be so inferior in quality that they disintegrated after only two or three weeks of use.[42]

A portion of each Sunday morning was reserved for inspection of the troops. When assembly was sounded the entire garrison fell out in full dress uniform to be reviewed by the post commander. Officers who were absent from the ranks or who failed to pass inspection were severely reprimanded by the commanding officer, while enlisted men who were guilty of the same lapses of military conduct were usually given extra duty.[43]

The Officer's Duty Day

A major portion of each day was filled with administrative duties for the post's officers. Boards were almost continually in session to act on court-martial proceedings or assess blame for shortages or waste in garrison supplies.[44] During periods of heavy desertion, captured violators were often required to wait several months before officers were available to convene court-martial hearings.[45]

Unlike the enlisted men, who were responsible only for the equipment directly issued to them, officers were charged with the care and retention of all government property held at the post. Officers were often brought before review boards of their peers to explain such allegations as having accepted contract beef that was too tough to eat, tainted bacon, rotten potatoes or wormy flour.[46] Hay stacks which were found to be short of the contracted tonnage upon inspection, or improperly piled so as not adequately to resist deterioration by rain and wind were the direct responsibility of the officer assigned to oversee the stacking process, and he could expect to be court-martialed or forced to pay for any loss incurred through his negligence.[47]

Similar recourse was taken when horses or mules were injured through the carelessness of an officer. Unless he could place the blame on another officer or an enlisted man, he was held responsible for any equipment that was lost or stolen during either garrison duty or scouts and marches in the field. The cost of the missing item was then to be deducted from the pay of the guilty party.[48] Thievery of government property by civilians who were either visiting or working at the post, became so serious at times that passes, which were issued only by the commanding officer, were required of all non-military personnel before they would be allowed to remain on the reservation.[49]

In addition to the regular line officers who commanded companies of infantry or cavalry, several officers were usually on post with special assignments. Included in this group were the chaplain, the post surgeon, the supply officer, the recruitment officer and, during periods when construction was underway, an army engineer or quartermaster officer.[50] Occasionally departmental staff officers visited the post for short periods to inspect the facilities or to serve as special procurement advisors. Whenever horses or mules were purchased at Fort Dodge, a military expert was sent to inspect the animals before they were accepted.[51]

Troop Procurement

The task of the post recruiter varied according to the immediate manpower needs of the garrison. When troop assignments from the Department of the Missouri were inadequate or during periods of unusually heavy desertion or enlistment expiration, the recruiter visited communities in eastern Kansas, hopeful of quickly filling the quota of needed men.[52] The size of newly assigned or recruited units varied from a few men to as many as two hundred.

The previous occupational backgrounds of recruits were so varied as to include men from almost every walk of life. On the rolls of a company of freshly organized soldiers of the United States 19th Infantry, which was sent to Fort Dodge in 1878, were eight bookkeepers, a former member of the Indiana Legislature, the son of an English nobleman, two ex-Confederate officers, one past member of the Confederate Congress, a railroad conductor, a former bank president whose liabilities had grown to exceed his assets, two medical students, two doctors, three school teachers and four merchants.[53]

When Indian outbreaks erupted unexpectedly after 1870, recruits were sought from the frontier towns close to the fort. Such special efforts to procure men were found to be necessary when the Department of the Missouri could not reinforce the garrison with added troops as quickly as was thought necessary.

As a last resort, military units were complemented with civilians during periods of crisis. In 1878, some seventy-five cowboys joined with the military to contest the passage of a group of Northern Cheyennes across the Arkansas River after they had broken out of their reservation in the Indian Territory.[54]

Garrison Indian Relations

The relationship of the garrison to the neighboring tribes of Indians was certainly not entirely confined to acts of mutual belligerency. Officers of the post occasionally mediated between opposing bands of Indians who had taken to the warpath to settle their differences.[55] On such instances the soldiers attempted to persuade the adversaries of the folly of war, in rather obvious contrast to their own function on the plains.

During the years which followed the Medicine Lodge Treaty of 1867, the section of that document which had denied the Indians the privilege of moving north of the Arkansas River was often temporarily suspended after the assurance had been given by their government agent that they intended only to hunt on the plains or trade with the post sutler.[56] The activity of the garrison was noticeably curtailed whenever Indians were camped near the post. Drill and skirmish practices were temporarily suspended as it was anticipated that the Indians might interpret such actions as evidence of impending attack and attempt to defend themselves. Enlisted men were denied passes from the post when Indians were present in the immediate area because bloodshed could easily result from troops fraternizing with the "comely ladies of the plains."[57]

As a result of one of his frequent visits to Fort Dodge during the spring of 1868, Satanta demonstrated to the garrison that he could be equally as troublesome during periods of peace as he was while on the warpath. The aggressive head chief of the Kiowas, still disgrunted over what he considered to have been discriminatory treatment the previous fall when his people were supposedly not given the same quantity or quality of goods as the other tribes at Medicine Lodge Creek, demanded that he be given food and whiskey from the supplies available at the post. Major Douglass responded by giving every man in Satanta's small party ten days' rations, but refused to provide them with the hoped-for whiskey.[58]

Shortly thereafter Satanta entered Douglass's quarters while he was not present and emptied a full bottle of El Paso wine. Encouraged by his initial success and by then thoroughly intoxicated, he went to the quarters of another officer and drank a bottle of extract of sarsaparilla. His search for alcohol then led him to the post stables, where he seized from a shelf a bottle which he presumed to be whiskey and promptly emptied it. Unfortunately the last bottle contained a physic remedy that had been readied for a sick horse. Shortly thereafter, Satanta suffered the same violent results that might have been anticipated had the animal been given the medicine.[59]

The embittered chieftain, thoroughly convinced that the officers of the post had tried to poison him, summoned his companions and after vowing vengeance on his tormentors, had left the fort. While he was returning to the village of his people south of the Arkansas River, he came across a party of white men, and after killing one of them, he took the horses, mules, clothing and bedding of the others and then rode on.

Upon reaching his encampment, Satanta summoned the Kiowa agent and demanded that he notify the Department of the Missouri of his gross mistreatment at Fort Dodge. He readily admitted the attack on the camp of white men; however, he pointed out that they were trespassing on reservation lands and he, therefore, had been justified in punishing them.[60]

When Major Douglass was later asked by his departmental superiors for an explanation of Satanta's charges, he pleaded the innocence of both himself and of his men to the suggestion they had deliberately allowed Satanta to drink the horse physic. He recommended that no punitive action be taken against the Kiowas in response to the attack on the trespassers, but he warned that renewed hostilities would be expected by late spring from the increasing belligerent reservation tribes south of the Arkansas River.[61]

Scouts and Marches in the Field

Because Fort Dodge was the most southwesterly post on the Kansas frontier, the garrison was charged with the task of guarding the entire line of Arkansas River from central Kansas as far west as Granada in Colorado Territory.[62] Scouting detachments were kept in the field almost continually along this line. The vigilant patrols often moved as far as one hundred miles north of the river line to search for hostiles or escapees from the southern reservations.[63] Approximately twenty-five thousand square miles of prairie were included in the area to be guarded by the fort.

Cavalry detachments covered on an average of twenty miles each day and usually remained in the field for from one to four weeks before returning to Fort Dodge for new orders, rest, fresh mounts and supplies.[64] Each man carried with him his field equipment and from fifty to one hundred rounds of ammunition.[65] Supplies were loaded on wagons that followed in the wake of the column of troops. A point rider and several flankers were sent approximately five hundred yards to the front and to each side of the advancing column to avoid surprise attack.[66]

When hostile Indians were reported operating near the line of march, the pace of movement was quickened to as much as fifty miles each day.[67] Such forced marches placed the cavalry in a difficult position once the enemy had been sighted. If the march had lasted for more than a few hours the horses were tired, and further pursuit of the Indians mounted on their swift and hardened ponies usually proved fruitless unless the adversary could be forced to stand and fight.[68]

These long marches and exhausting rides were difficult for veteran troopers and physical nightmares for new cavalry recruits. Inexperience on such scouts could easily lead to such mistakes as allowing a horse to step in prairie dog holes or rodent burrows, thereby throwing and often seriously injuring the rider.[69] Officers frequently complained bitterly that their effectiveness on marches was often greatly reduced by the inadequate training given cavalry recruits before they were assigned to field duty.[70]

Occasionally officers pushed their commands too hard in pursuit of Indians and their mounts gave out, leaving many of the men on foot. On one such instance, during the spring of 1869, a detachment of the United States Tenth Cavalry, which was scouting the area north of Fort Dodge, pursued a band of Indians for several days and then found it necessary to shoot eighty of their horses who had become "lived out" by the strain of the chase.[71]

The post surgeon at Fort Dodge reported that the men were fed poorly on scouts and marches and often acquired scurvy as a result of the lack of fresh food, yet they seldom complained of illness while in the field as they feared the ridicule of their fellow soldiers.[72] Whenever the line of march moved a detachment near one of the "whiskey ranches" that dotted the prairie, fresh food and liquor could be enjoyed by the men.[73] Although a number of officers and enlisted men filled their canteens with whiskey before departing on a march, their flasks were soon emptied on the prairie, and the chance to replenish their exhausted supply of spirits was generally welcomed.[74]

Occasionally soldiers who lacked the funds to purchase whiskey traded stolen government property for their liquor, thereby inviting reprisal on the "whiskey ranches" by the commander of Fort Dodge. After one detachment had traded the forage they carried for their animals for whiskey, the incensed post commander ordered a second detachment to ride to the ranch and destroy the remaining supply of alcohol.[75]

Friendly bands of Indians who left their reservations in the Indian Territory to hunt buffalo on the Kansas prairies without their agents' permission were escorted south of the Arkansas River when they were intercepted by patrols. If the Indians were obviously hungry, the detachments were often permitted to purchase cattle for them to eat after they had returned to their reservation.[76]

The Duty of Civilian Scouts

A number of civilians were regularly employed by the post to serve as scouts, guides and interpreters. During periods of relative peace, only five to ten men were employed for such duty; however, twenty to thirty scouts were often hired preceding a general campaign.[77] Each scout was provided with a horse, weapons and field equipment by the government, but the costs of lost equipment or horses that had been "ridden down" without a valid cause were deducted from their pay.[78]

Scouts who were assigned to garrison duty were required to ride out from the post each morning one hour before sunrise and inspect the vicinity immediately surrounding the fort. After the area close to the post had been searched, the scouts returned to the fort and reported anything suspicious they had observed to the chief of scouts. Shortly after reveille the scouts returned to the field; the second inspection of the area carried the men out four to five miles from the post.[79]

Once a military detachment was in the field the service of the scouts became crucial to the success or failure of the mission. Their duties included setting the line of march, procuring fresh meat, investigating the area surrounding the command for ambushes, searching for suitable fording areas across streams, finding water, locating the trails of Indians, and conversing with them to ascertain their motives if they were found to be hostile.[80]

Faulty intelligence reports could prove most costly and embarrassing to the military. It was later suspected that the chief of scouts at Fort Dodge during the winter of 1867, Fred F. Jones, had purposefully exaggerated his reports that the Cheyennes and Sioux were planning to join the southern tribes in a general uprising during the spring. Jones's reports which had been immediately forwarded to departmental headquarters and finally to the Secretary of War, were admittedly instrumental in the decision that was reached by the latter to send Hancock onto the plains during the spring of 1867. The unfortunate burning of the Cheyenne village might have been averted if Jones's reports of intended hostilities had been more accurate.[81] Oddly enough, Jones was later hired to scout for Fort Hays after he had been dismissed from service at Fort Dodge.

During the spring of 1868, it was found that several of the scouts at Fort Dodge were involved in stealing horses from the Indians. Investigation of the matter failed to separate the innocent from the guilty and the entire contingent was relieved of duty and replaced by an entirely new group of scouts.[82]

When no hostile bands of Indians were known to be in the area surrounding the Fort Dodge post, dispatches were generally carried by enlisted men; however, because of their superior horsemanship and knowledge of the terrain to be traveled, scouts were asked to carry the messages if the task was considered hazardous. If it was anticipated that the man carrying dispatches would quite likely be attacked along the route by Indians, bounties were offered to volunteers willing to risk the ride. For those missions that were considered only moderately dangerous, the bounty was usually twenty-five dollars;[83] but if it was anticipated that the scout's chances of being killed were unusually high, the bounty was increased to as much as one hundred dollars.[84]

Military Field Service to the Frontier

One of the most demanding tasks assigned to the Fort Dodge garrison was that of providing relief to besieged or stranded wagon trains traveling the Santa Fe Trail. Cavalry patrols scouted the route continually during periods of Indian uprisings; and if attack was imminent, infantrymen accompanied the trains along the trail.[85] In spite of the vigilance of the fort, a number of successful raids were carried out by the Indians yearly from 1865 until 1878.

Once an attack was reported to the post, detachments were sent to the beleagured train as quickly as possible. In most cases the Indians broke off their attack on the approach of the military rather than contest their prize with so dangerous an adversary.[86] Other trains could be raided later, and perhaps the troopers would not arrive until the wagons had been completely overrun.

Trains that were reasonably well armed could usually hold off the enemy, but few emerged from such conflicts without having forfeited most of their draft animals. The noise of battle was usually punctuated with shrill outcries by the Indians which were intended to frighten the stock. The usual result was the stampeding and loss of the teams.[87] Occasionally bands of Indians that had captured the teams of a train, but feared they could not overrun the wagons before help arrived, attempted under a flag of truce to barter with the wagon-master, offering to exchange the animals for goods carried on the wagons.

Stranded trains were pulled to safety with mules sent out from Fort Dodge when they were available, but the post herd often did not have an adequate number of animals available for such service, thereby necessitating the posting of a military guard with the wagons until such time as stock could be provided.[88] One stranded train in 1868 proved, at least temporarily, to be a soldier's dream. The train had lost all of its stock during a raid near the Cimarron, and the detachment of troops sent out to guard the wagons soon found that a major portion of the cargo was kegged whiskey. The Mexican wagonmaster, grateful for the protection afforded by the troopers, generously shared the liquor with the soldiers. Unfortunately before the wagons could be hauled to safety several days later, a number of intoxicated soldiers and wagon hands were involved in a general shooting melee, during which several men lost their lives.[89]

The disgusted commander of the fort, Major John H. Page, sent a second detachment of cavalry to the train armed with axes and under orders to empty the remaining kegs of whiskey. The infuriated owner of the train, J. Francisco Chavez, a prominent New Mexican merchant and a personal friend of General Grant, complained to the Department of War that his property had been maliciously destroyed without just cause. Page was subsequently called upon by the Department of the Missouri to explain his actions; however, no formal charges were drawn up against the major after he replied that he had ordered the whiskey destroyed only upon gathering evidence that some of the liquor had been sold to the troops. As none of the Mexicans were licensed to retail whiskey in Kansas, the officer cleverly pleaded that he had no recourse other than to stave in the remaining kegs.[90]

The rather rash action of the major was undoubtedly initiated by several similar incidents which had taken place at the Cimarron in the past. Detachments that were bivouacked near the crossing during the season of heavy travel frequently shared the liquor of passing trains and had often been found in a state of drunkenness by inspecting officers.[91] If it was difficult to keep the men from the whiskey, it was perhaps more feasible to keep the whiskey from the men.

In addition to guarding the commercial routes of western Kansas, the garrison provided police protection for the frontier communities which were being built near the fort by 1870. Bands of horse and cattle thieves preyed on the ranches of the area as well as in the Indian Territory to the south. The thieves often established bogus ranches on which they gathered considerable herds of stolen stock that was later driven east for sale.[92] These bands frequently numbered as many as ten or twenty men and ranged as far as two hundred miles from their base of operation in search of animals to rustle.[93]

Few frontier towns possessed enough law officers to engage so formidable an adversary, thereby necessitating that the military assume the responsibility for their capture. Cavalry detachments often trailed stolen herds for several days before the thieves could be caught. A number of soldiers lost their lives skirmishing with cornered bands of outlaws.[94] On one occasion a bold group of thieves rustled the post beef herd; however, they gave up the stock and fled without contesting the issue upon the approach of a pursuing unit of cavalry.[95]

In 1878, during the later years of the post's existence, troops were sent into the field to search for Dave Rudabaugh's gang of train robbers, who had struck at the nearby town of Kinsley. On this occasion the soldiers could not find the thieves, but they were later apprehended by a Dodge City posse led by Sheriff William Barclay "Bat" Masterson.[96]

As the settler's frontier pressed forward to surround the fort during the late 1870's, the garrison was forced to guard the reservation from trespassers who either allowed their livestock to graze on the fort's land or cut down timber from the military groves. If initial warnings were unheeded, chronic violators were arrested and forced to pay for the damage inflicted on the reservation.[97]

The open expanses of prairie grass near the post were a constant source of danger from fires that could travel several miles per hour when driven along by the prevailing high winds of western Kansas. When fires were sighted, troopers were sent out to warn settlers in the path, and several wagons from the post were loaded with men supplied with wet burlap sacks and shovels to fight the blaze with backfires until it could be contained.[98]

During the unusually severe winter that struck Kansas in 1874, the post distributed food and clothing to destitute settlers along the frontier. The blizzards followed in the wake of a summer of drought that had parched the crops of the area, leaving hundreds of families without food for the winter months. In addition to the distribution of rations, thousands of blankets, shoes and articles of clothing were handed out to the needy.[99]

An infrequent opportunity for relief from the monotony of plains soldiering was provided for four companies of troops from the fort in 1877, when they were ordered to St. Louis, Missouri, to help quell the railroad strike that was convulsing that city.[100] However, the aftermath of the trip was less than pleasant for many of the soldiers. A number of them had contracted venereal disease while not combating strikes, and they spent a good portion of the following winter in the post hospital under the rather unsympathetic treatment of Dr. William S. Tremaine, the fort's surgeon.[101]

Leisure and Recreation

When the troops of Fort Dodge were not in the field or assigned to garrison guard duty, the hours from 6:00 P.M. until 9:30 P.M., were available for relaxation and diversion from the routine of military life. The post recreation

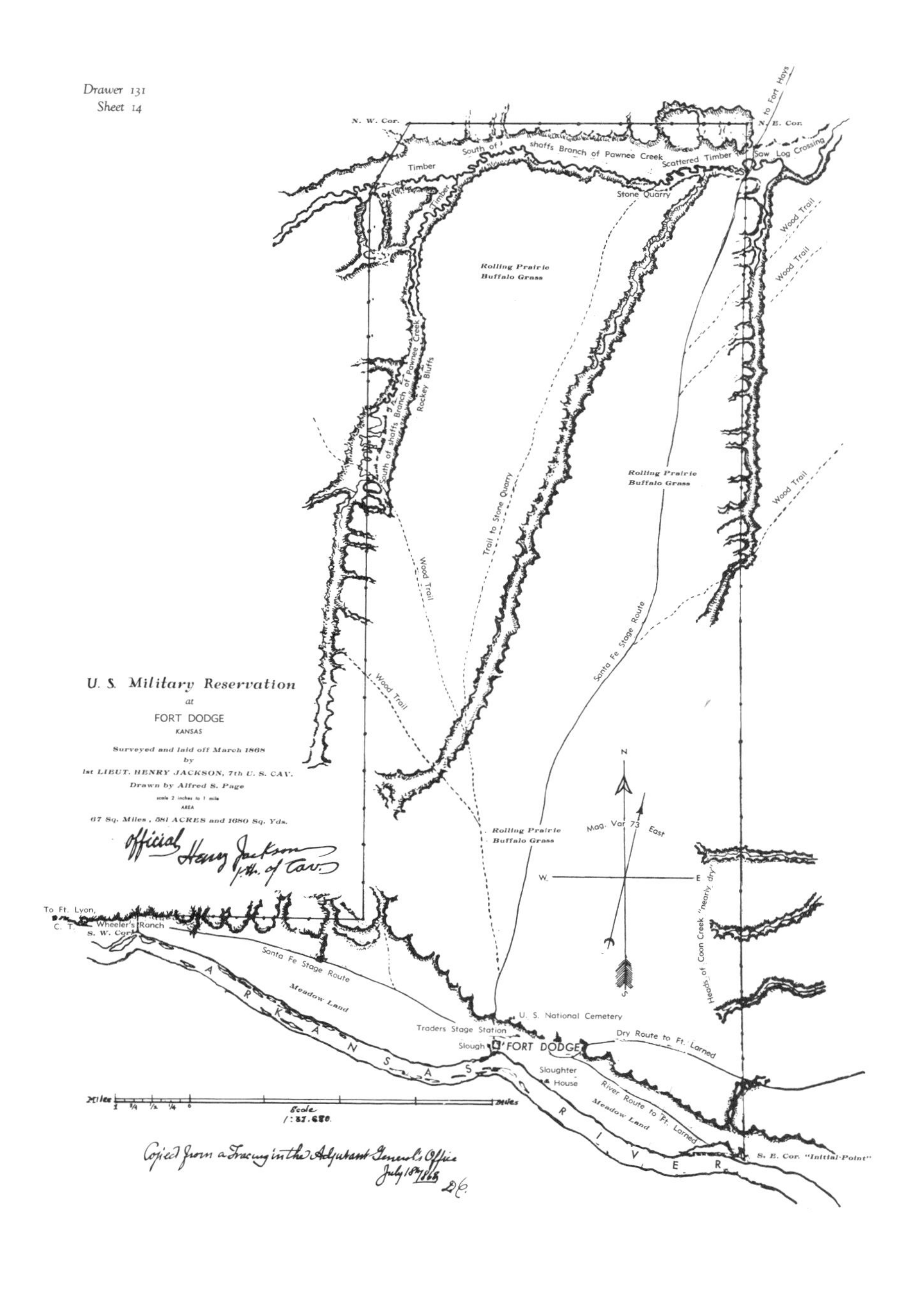
Drawer 131
Sheet 14
N. W. Cor.
N. E. Cor.
to Fort Hays
Timber
South of
shaffs Branch of Pawnee Creek
Scattered Timber
Saw Log Crossing
Stone Quarry
Timber
Wood Trail
Wood Trail
Rolling Prairie
Buffalo Grass
South of shaffs Branch of Pawnee Creek
Rockey Bluffs
Trail to Stone Quarry
Rolling Prairie
Buffalo Grass
Wood Trail
Wood Trail
Santa Fe Stage Route
Wood Trail
U. S. Military Reservation
at
FORT DODGE
KANSAS
Surveyed and laid off March 1868
by
1st LIEUT. HENRY JACKSON, 7th U. S. CAV.
Drawn by Alfred S. Page
scale 2 inches to 1 mile
AREA
67 Sq. Miles, 581 ACRES and 1680 Sq. Yds.
Official Henry Jackson 1st Lt. of Cav.
Rolling Prairie
Buffalo Grass
N
Mag. Var 73 East
W.
E
S
Heads of Coon Creek "nearly dry"
To Ft. Lyon,
C. T.
Wheeler's Ranch
S. W. Cor.
Santa Fe Stage Route
Meadow Land
ARKANSAS RIVER
U. S. National Cemetery
Traders Stage Station
Slough
FORT DODGE
Dry Route to Ft. Larned
Slaughter House
River Route to Ft. Larned
Meadow Land
Miles
Miles
Scale
1:31.680
S. E. Cor. "Initial Point"
Copied from a Tracing in the Adjutant General's Office
July 18th 1868

Kansas State Soldiers Home
Fort Dodge

GEN. GRENVILLE M. DODGE

The nation's treatment of the Indians persuaded the General that "The policy of the United States is beyond the comprehension of any sensible man. In all the days of Indian warfare and treaties, there never was such a farce or failure to comprehend the frontier situation as that of 1865 and 1866."

U. S. Army Fort Sill Museum

CHIEF SATANTA

The heavy hearted Kiowa lamented that the advancing frontier of the white man "takes our grass, our wood, our wild game and our water, and we are given nothing in return."

QUANAH PARKER
A Kwahadi Commanche Chieftain born of a captive white woman and a Commanche warrior, he led his tribesmen in a last desperate defense of the remnants of the southern buffalo herd as they were being slaughtered by hunters.

Western History Collections
University of Oklahoma Library

DULL KNIFE
A Cheyenne Indian's reply, 1875, to an order to return to the reservation.

Photograph of pen drawing
by Maynard Dixon

Western History Collections
University of Oklahoma Library

GROUND PLAN of FORT DODGE,

KANSAS

ESTABLISHED 1864

Latitude, 37° 48' 16" N. Longitude 99° 56' W.

MATERIALS OF BUILDINGS

□ STONE, CONSTRUCTED IN 1867

△ ADOBE, 1868

WOOD 1870-77

FOR DIMENSIONS and COSTS of CONSTRUCTION (WHERE KNOWN) SEE OUTLINES OF BUILDINGS

ICE HOUSE
30 x 55

DEAD HOUSE
10 x 12
$38.50

STORE ROOM
26 x 40
$450.⁰⁰

C. O. STABLE
18 x 24

TRADER STORE

DETACHED WARD
24 x 76

HOSPITAL
10 x 18
30 x 67
30 x 40

OFFICERS
24 x 40
24 x 40

COMDG OFFICER
16 x 22
30 x 52

QUARTERS
24 x 40

OFFICERS QUARTERS
32
22' 6"

LIBRARY
14 x 20

$781.47
16 x 32
LAUNDRESSES

$781.47
16 x 32
POST SCHOOL

BARRACKS
30 x 130
26 x 52

WASH-HOUSE
16 x 24

BARRACKS
30 x 130
26 x 52

WASH-HOUSE
16 x 24

BARRACKS
30 x 130
26 x 52

WASH-HOUSE
16 x 24

$781.47
16 x 32
$781.47
16 x 32
LAUNDRESSES

Variation 15° East

CAVALRY CORRAL
68 x 220

POST TRAIN CORRAL, QMD
68 x 220

SHED

FIELD TRAIN CORRAL QMD
200 x 220
$1,59429/160

TEAMSTERS QRTS SADDLER
16 x 30 16 x 28 16 x 18

TEAMSTERS QRS
16 x 20

CORRAL MASTER
14 x 16

Audjt's office
30
28
$319.25

MAGAZINE
18 x 18
$973.47

GUARD HOUSE
36 x 50

GRANARY
30 x 110
$1381.41

WARE HOUSE
SUBS. 31 x 130
Q.M. 25 x 106
Q.M. 31 x 130

BAKE HOUSE
24 x 56

BUTCHER SHOP
17 x 28

COMMS'Y SERGT'S QRS.
32 x 14

ORD. SERGT'S QRS.
32 x 14

BLACKSMITH'S & W. W. SHOPS
90 x 25 $752.87

CARPENTER SHOP
30 x 22

OLD B.S. SHOP

ARKANSAS RIVER

Kansas State Soldiers Home
Fort Dodge

DODGE CITY

The lusty little cow town had grown so tarnished in 1878 that the local newspaper predicted, "When Gabriel blows his horn a motley crowd of sinners will send forth from Boot Hill to attend the final judgment."

[illegible], CHIEF OF THE KIOWAS. — SET-IM-KA-YE, OR "STUMBLING BEAR." — TEN-E-AU-COOP, OR "KICKING BIRD."

THE INDIAN WAR.

THE news from the HANCOCK and SULLY expeditions against the hostile Indians is to May [illegible]. The councils which have been held have not resulted in a permanent peace; but, on the contrary, war has become general throughout the Territories occupied by the Cheyennes, Sioux, Kiowas, [illegible], and Apaches. General HANCOCK held councils with the Kiowas on April 24 at Fort Dodge, and on May 1 near Fort Larned. The Indians promised to remain at peace, but on May 4 they declared "war to the knife." General HANCOCK's answer was, "You shall have war until every warrior cries enough," and he immediately began active operations against them. The effect of his first movement from Fort Larned was the driving of the Cheyennes, who had been threatening the "Arkansas" and "Smoky Hill" routes to the northward. They moved in four large war-parties, and appeared on the "Platte River" or "Northern Route" on May 7. They burned two ranches and committed other depredations. Meantime General SULLY, at Fort Laramie, was engaged in holding councils with the Indians from the Territories north of the Platte River, all of whom professed a desire for peace. Lieutenant-General SHERMAN, commanding in the West, repaired to Fort Harker on May 11, for the purpose of holding a final talk with the Kiowas, Comanches, Cheyennes, and Arapahoes, in the hope of patching up a peace.

Our illustrations in this connection are of more than usual interest. The "Council at Fort Dodge," on April 24, was held in a Sibley tent, and Generals HANCOCK and A. J. SMITH, Colonels WYNCOOP, LEAVENWORTH, and MITCHELL, and Major DOUGLASS, and DICK CURTIS, the interpreter, were present. The Indians were represented by TEN-E-AU-COOP, or "Kicking Bird," a portrait of whom we give, and who is described by our artist as "the shrewdest scoundrel of the Kiowas." He affects the costume of

INDIAN COUNCIL AT FORT DODGE, KANSAS, BETWEEN GENERAL HANCOCK AND THE KIOWA CHIEFS.—[SKETCHED BY THEODORE R. DAVIS.]

INTERIOR OF FORT DODGE, KANSAS.—[SKETCHED BY THEODORE R. DAVIS.]

the whites, and wears a soldier's uniform if he can get it. SET-AM-GA-KE, or "Stumbling Bear," who was also present, appears to be a rival of "Kicking Bird," as our artist calls him "the *greatest* scoundrel of the Kiowa tribe." Probably the only mode of describing individuals of the race is to give their relative degrees in villainy. ALTELA is looked upon by the army officers as a true friend of peace, but in the council, on this occasion, his opinion appears to have had little weight with his red brethren. The council near Fort Larned on May 1 was held with SA-TAC-TI, one of the Kiowa chiefs; but it resulted like the rest—only in promises of peace.

We also give a view of the "Interior of Fort Dodge," a post on the "Smoky Hill Route," which was established about three years ago. Its garrison consists of about one hundred soldiers of all arms. The quarters of the officers are sunk in the ground to the depth of three or four feet. The rest of the structure is of sod, plastered inside and out. The roofs are composed of small saplings, on which bushes are thrown and covered with earth.

The "Sutler's Store at Fort Dodge" shows the interior of the lounging-place for all the idlers about the station—it is, in fact, the grand hotel, restaurant, and club-house of the post. After the 1st of July next the act of Congress abolishing the post of sutler goes into operation, and these very convenient pests of an army, the sutlers, go out.

SUTLER'S STORE AT FORT DODGE, KANSAS.—[SKETCHED BY THEODORE R. DAVIS.]

FORT DODGE AS A MATURE POST, ABOUT 1878

The primary task of the post at this date included keeping a watchful eye on the Indian Territory to the south, and patroling the frontier around Dodge City.

Kansas State Soldiers Home
Fort Dodge

Western History Collections
University of Oklahoma Library

The stone barracks proved so durable that a century after they had been completed in 1867, the buildings were still being used.

U.S. ARMY-INFANTRY ATTACKED BY INDIANS-1876

CUSTER'S CHARGE ON BLACK KETTLE'S VILLAGE

Western History Collections
University of Oklahoma Library

At dawn on November 26, 1868, Custer's 7th Cavalry charged into the sleeping village of Black Kettle's Southern Cheyenne, carrying out his orders to the letter.

Drawn for this publication
Mary L. Schnoebelen

BLACK KETTLE

As a chieftain of the Southern Cheyennes, Black Kettle dedicated much of his adult life to securing peace for his people. In the end he fell at the Washita under the charge of Custer's Seventh Cavalry.

LITTLE RAVEN, WILL BENT, AND LITTLE RAVEN'S SONS
Fort Dodge, Kansas, August 5, 1869

One of the West's most respected and effective contacts with the southern tribes, Will Bent died shortly after this visit to Fort Dodge in 1869, at the height of the final struggle for the Plains.

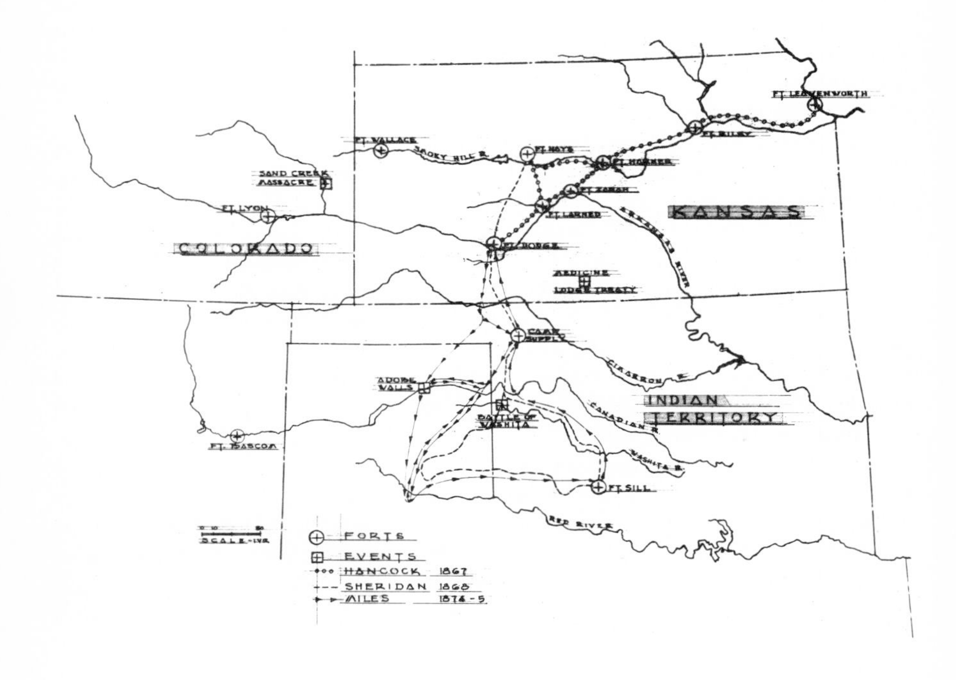

FORT DODGE AND THE PLAINS INDIAN CAMPAIGNS

hall contained a billiards table and a card table as well as a modest library.[102] Although the post commander denied the charge made by the fort's chaplain to departmental headquarters that he knowingly tolerated gambling in the hall, he did not question the possibility that money was changing hands through the fate of poker games that were played there. He pleaded that neither he nor any other officer on the post could be reasonably expected to curtail gambling completely on the grounds of the fort if the men were determined to play. If the recreation hall was closed to card playing, the barracks or the stables would serve equally well.[103]

In addition to a limited number of books which were available in the library, the post subscribed to several magazines and newspapers for enjoyment of the garrison. After Dodge City was established near the fort in 1872, the fort contributed to the town's newspaper a column that served to enlighten the surrounding community on the current military and social activities of the post.[104]

The most popular center of relaxation during off-duty hours was the post sutler's store. Whiskey could be purchased there by both military and civilian personnel, but the hours during which liquor could be sold to enlisted men were closely regulated. The bar was not permitted to open until six-thirty in the evening, and it had to be closed following the blowing of taps at 9:30 P.M.[105]

Drunkenness was a chronic problem at the fort, and various post commanders tried several methods of limiting the consumption of alcohol. One of Fort Dodge's commanding officers limited the sale of liquor to three drinks per evening to each man; however, the sutler apparently often lost count as drunkenness continued to plague the post.[106] Whiskey was never to be sold to a man who was obviously already under the influence of spirits, but it was admittedly difficult for the sutler to judge when a man had consumed a permissible amount of liquor.

On several occasions the sale of whiskey to enlisted men was suspended, yet the bar was never closed to officers.[107] These periods of prohibition were usually short lived as the commanding officers were for the most part aware of the limited recreation available on the military frontier and therefore sympathetic to the desire of the men to enjoy the fellowship of their comrades over a few drinks. The sutler's bar was closed to enlisted men briefly during the summer of 1872, when the Officer of the Day discovered that the entire mail escort, which was about to leave for Camp Supply in the Indian Territory, was so intoxicated they could not ride their horses.[108]

On another occasion the post surgeon found that whiskey was being smuggled into the hospital. He complained to the post commander that he could hardly be expected to nurse the men back to health if they were consuming considerable quantities of alcohol during the course of treatment.[109]

Of all the officers who commanded the fort, perhaps Colonel Richard I. Dodge was the most vehemently opposed to the sale of liquor to the garrison. Colonel Dodge served two tours of duty at the post, the first during the summer of 1872, the second including the first nine months of 1873. The colonel, who bore the illustrious Dodge name rather proudly, was considered by the men of the garrison to be a somewhat inflexible officer who "went by the book."

During his first tour at the post, the colonel had vigorously berated a colored lieutenant of the United States Tenth Cavalry he found drinking with the enlisted men of his company. The incensed lieutenant struck Colonel Dodge, knocking him down, and after mounting his horse, rode through the post recreation room, firing several shots from his revolver through the sutler's store. He was soon subdued by a blow on the head with a billiard cue.[110]

Colonel Dodge petitioned the Department of the Missouri in 1872, to extend the fort's military reservation several miles southward because "rumshops and houses of ill repute" were being built on the south side of the Arkansas River, where the military had no jurisdiction. The colonel advised his superiors that constant trouble could be expected unless the men of the garrison were denied the opportunity of frequenting the newly established businesses. Because the river stood between the fort and the "rum shops and houses of ill repute," thus curtailing the patronage their proprietors could expect from the nearby garrison, the establishments were moved across the boundary of the southwestern extremity of the military reservation. There, still in 1872, they were formed into the town of Dodge City.[111]

In addition to the pastime of drinking, card games and music could be enjoyed at the sutler's store. The soldiers frequently danced to the strains of the sutler's musicians; however, they were usually forced to rely on a fellow soldier as a dancing partner.[112] On festive occasions balls were held at the fort, with attendance usually restricted to the officers and their wives.[113]

Nature's generous stocking of game near the fort encouraged the troops to hunt and fish when they were not on duty. During the early years of the post's existence buffalo, antelope, wolves, coyotes, rabbits and numerous game birds were readily available to the hunter, but the prevalence of all these species declined sharply after the settler's frontier had moved westward to encircle the fort. The soldiers were perhaps as guilty as the later inhabitants of the plains as participants in the slaughter of the animals and birds of the prairie.[114] The supply seemed so invitingly inexhaustible that army generals, Eastern sportsmen, prominent politicians and foreign gentlemen often journeyed to Fort Dodge to share in the unusually fine hunting that was available.

Several of the officers of the garrison kept dogs, and English style hunts for coyotes or wolves proved to be quite popular.[115] One officer purchased several greyhounds to run down antelope; however, he was greatly disappointed with the result. Before they could be retrieved by their owner, the tenacious dogs literally ran themselves to death attempting to catch the fleet animals.[116]

The nearby river was well stocked with catfish, carp and buffalo fish. Occasionally mountain trout that had drifted downstream from the Colorado Territory were caught. The carpenters of the garrison built several boats for use of fishermen in 1869; but when the post commander was informed of their project, they were reprimanded for using time which should have been given to the renovation of the officers' quarters.[117]

A portion of the leisure hours of a number of the men was spent competing for the favors of the post laundresses. Each company was allowed to hire four women for this function, while a number of others were retained to serve the officers exclusively.[118] The wages paid these women indicate that their expected duties extended beyond the washboard. The enlisted men who did not do their own laundry or hire it done on a piece basis were charged six dollars per month for the services of a laundress.[119] If only a few of the men availed themselves of the women's services, the cost would have been considerable. The six dollar fee represented almost half of the enlisted private's pay.

The laundresses usually moved from post to post with the men when they were transferred.[120] At Fort Dodge they were initially placed in dugouts that had been made available after the enlisted men moved into permanent barracks; however, during later years they were provided with more suitable quarters.[121]

On one occasion a colonel who had been ordered to report to Camp Supply from Fort Hays asked the commander at Fort Dodge to provide private transportation for his two personal laundresses to his newly assigned station. When the irritated commander reported the request to his departmental superiors, the colonel was severely reprimanded, whereupon he informed the Fort Dodge officer that he would certainly never rely on his personal discretion in the future.[122]

The brazenness of the laundresses occasionally necessitated that the post commander restrict the latitude of their duties. Orders were periodically issued reminding the enlisted men that all military personnel were expected to sleep in their own quarters,[123] while the laundresses were ejected from the officers' quarters when it became apparent that they were spending their nights as well as their days improving the comfort of the officers.[124]

Military Discipline

The spectrum of offenses committed by the troops of Fort Dodge that were punishable by court-martial varied from rather minor breaches of conduct, such as walking on the grass of the parade ground, fighting, swearing or drunkenness, to the most serious military crimes, which included damaging, destroying or stealing government property, and cowardice in the field. Undoubtedly the most prevalent of all major offenses among the enlisted men was desertion from the garrison.[125]

Officers were most frequently summoned before a board of their peers to answer charges that they had failed to protect adequately the military property or stores for which they were responsible. On less numerous occasions they were disciplined for personal conduct in violation of the military code established for those holding commissions or because of disputes which had originated over rank and privilege of command.[126]

A board of inquiry was usually assembled to weigh the evidence of serious charges and judge whether or not the accused should later be brought before a formal court-martial hearing.[127] Five officers were called to review the testimony given at such hearings; however, the trials of officers serving the fort were usually transferred to a sister post to avoid bias on the part of the court.[128] The decisions of these boards were final unless an error in trial procedure was later detected by a superior review board. In such cases a new hearing was invariably ordered.

Few court-martial proceedings were so fortunate as to include such an impeccable judge as handed down the decision at Fort Dodge during a trial in the spring of 1873. The board had been called to hear a dispute over the right to command between two officers with the identical rank and time in grade who were serving at a sister fort. During the course of the proceedings one of the officers died and the trial records duly noted that the issue had been settled by the "highest authority" possible.[129]

The smoldering feud which had initially erupted between Major Douglass and Chaplain White in 1868 over the part time use of the post recreation hall as a school and church finally led to such serious charges and countercharges by the antagonists that both were summoned before a board of inquiry at Topeka, Kansas, to settle the dispute. The post commander accused the chaplain of neglecting his educational and spiritual duties while utilizing his personal quarters to merchandise trade goods obtained from two former sutlers at the fort. Both of these men had been ordered to move off the premises when it became obvious they were taking advantage of the troops of the garrison by selling inferior goods at exorbitant prices.[130]

The major also asked that the chaplain be censured for his unethical motives in petitioning the Department of the Missouri to reduce the military reservation of Fort Dodge to four square miles. He charged that Major White was in league with a group of civilians who planned to seize and operate the fort's stone quarry as soon as the site was vacated by the garrison. The chaplain was supposedly acting in anticipation of a lucrative business in the sale of quarried stone once the settler's rapidly approaching frontier had moved that far west.[131]

The chaplain responded by accusing the major and several of his staff officers of selling whiskey to the Indians.[132] Major White was found guilty as charged and permitted to resign his commission.[133] Although Douglass and his fellow officers were exonerated of the charges brought against them, the post commander chose to resign his commission and terminate his military career.

Douglass's tour as post commander had been unusually trying. The pressures of building a permanent post, negotiating with the Indians, and attempting to protect the frontier with the inadequate number of troops at his disposal had left the major somewhat embittered. In May of 1869, he notified his fellow officers at Fort Dodge of his decision and advised his friends that in the future he could be reached as H. E. Douglass, Esquire, Vice-President of Hazard Powder Company, Corner of Wall and Water Streets, New York City, New York.[134]

At times men resorted to the use of firearms to settle their disputes. In 1870, a captain who was displeased with the derogatory testimony regarding his personal character given before a board of inquiry by a fellow officer, confronted his accuser at the post sutler's store and after a brief argument drew a derringer pistol and fired. Although the men were standing only four feet apart, the bullet fortunately struck a pocket watch carried in the victim's shirt, thereby undoubtedly saving his life.[135]

Because of the crudeness and general inadequacy of the post guard house, the officers of the post frequently hesitated to bring court-martial proceedings against soldiers unless they stood accused of a serious crime. The frame structure measured only eighteen by twenty-eight feet, and even though it was reserved for the worst offenders, an average of eighteen men were held in the guard house at all times awaiting trial or transfer to a military prison.[136]

The guard house at Fort Larned was similar to the structure at Fort Dodge, and prisoners frequently escaped from both posts. When one garrison allowed captured deserters of the other to escape, as was frequently the case, a series of discourteous notes would be exchanged berating the military efficiency of the other fort.[137]

The unsightly, cold and unsanitary guard house remained a post facility until 1874, when General Sheridan noticed the structure while inspecting the post. The general notified the Department of the Missouri that the building was "disgraceful" and asked that funds be forwarded as soon as possible for the construction of a suitable building.[138]

Minor lapses of discipline, such as public swearing, fighting or drunkenness, often brought fines of from two and one-half to ten dollars.[139] Conviction of guilt for even a minor offense usually resulted in forfeiture of rank.[140] Habitual offenders usually drew a tour of duty at hard labor in addition to loss of rank and a fine.[141] Garrison tasks assigned as extra duty included tending the blacksmith shop, cleaning the latrines and collecting garbage in the post "slop wagon." The quarry, kiln, hay meadows and timber reserves provided disciplinary labor off the post.

On an average approximately five to ten percent of the garrison was absent without leave at all times.[142] During seasons of heavy scouting, marching and campaigning, such as occurred in 1867, 1868 and 1874, desertions often exceeded twenty-five percent of the total command.[143] The high incidence of desertion was certainly not unique with troops of Fort Dodge. Her sister posts along both the Santa Fe and Smoky Hill Routes were plagued with a similar problem.[144]

Deserters often took a horse, rations and their weapons with them, but they usually discarded the tell-tale army uniform as quickly as possible. Those who left on foot during the early years of the post's service often timed their flight so that they might find passage to eastern Kansas or New Mexico on a nearby wagon train.[145] Almost certain death awaited those found afoot on the open prairie by Indians. A number of deserters froze to death attempting to escape during the grip of winter.[146]

As soon as the absence of soldiers was detected, descriptions of the missing men were sent to every military post and town in the vicinity of the fort. This procedure was reciprocal, and the posts of western Kansas spent almost as much time hunting those missing from other forts as they did seeking their own deserters.

The task of accompanying deserters back to Fort Dodge was often hazardous work for the men given the assignment. A second attempt at flight could be expected if the opportunity should present itself. The prisoners were well aware of the military discipline awaiting them at the fort. One soldier chose suicide as an alternative to returning to military life.[147] In 1868 a sergeant was awarded the Congressional Medal of Honor for meritorious conduct while returning a deserter to Fort Dodge. He had fought off the efforts of several civilian friends of the prisoner to free his charge and had returned the man to the post guard house to await trial.[148]

Once a deserter escaped from the area immediately surrounding the fort, the chances of apprehending him were slight. A significant number of those who enlisted in the army entered the service with an assumed name, and if they chose to leave their company it was difficult to identify them in public from the meager description supplied by the garrison.[149]

A standing reward of thirty dollars was offered for the capture and delivery of a deserter to the nearest military post.[150] Ironically, the bounty for stolen or lost horses was considerably more, often as much as one hundred twenty-five dollars.[151] Civilians of western Kansas, frequently short of cash because of poor crops or pressing land mortgages, often sought deserters for the promised reward.[152] These bounty hunters were resented by the troops of the garrison, and on one occasion the guards on duty at the fort stood by and watched as a deserter beat his captors with a shovel after he had been released to their custody.[153]

The punishment handed down to deserters by court-martial boards varied considerably. If the unauthorized absence was for only a short period, and if the guilty party gave himself up, or if the soldier was considered to be genuinely remorseful for his act of disobedience, he might be ordered to serve only sixty or ninety days in the guard house. The usual punishment, however, was forfeiture of pay and rank, dishonorable discharge from the army and from six months to one year's confinement at hard labor at the Fort Leavenworth Military Prison.[154]

One of the most exacting sentences was meted out to Private Isaac Frisby of the United States Tenth Cavalry, who had deserted while his company was in the field campaigning against the Indians in 1869. Private Frisby was ordered to forfeit all pay, except for outstanding debts owed by him, was to be branded with an indelible vermillion letter D, two inches long, on his left hand, and after being dishonorably discharged from military service, he was to serve five years at hard labor at Fort Leavenworth.[155]

The Ill, the Wounded and the Dead

The most frequent illnesses afflicting the garrison were venereal disease, scurvy, frostbite, rabies, diarrhea, tuberculosis, alcoholism and pneumonia.[156] Although a number of the troops already suffered from venereal disease prior to their arrival at the fort, others contacted the disease from Indian women, post laundresses and after 1872 from prostitutes living at nearby Dodge City.[157]

Scurvy remained a chronic medical problem throughout the years of the post's service. The surgeons of Fort Dodge treated the disease by supplementing the monotonous diet of staples with pickles, dried fruit, cabbage, milk and buffalo meat, when beef was not available.[158]

Diarrhea was frequently the result of poor sanitary practices. The post surgeons periodically berated the troops for their general lack of cleanliness and warned them to boil the food they ate if they expected to remain free of the affliction.[159] Pneumonia and several related respiratory ailments were apparently contacted as a result of almost continual exposure to the elements. Winter marches in snow or rain and habitually cold barracks undoubtedly increased the prevalence of respiratory illnesses.[160]

Rabies took a surprisingly high toll of troops, often immediately following bivouacs in the field. Colonel Richard I. Dodge recalled awakening one morning while his command was camped at the Cimarron and finding that the nose of one of the soldiers had been severely gnawed during the night by a rabid skunk.[161] The disease driven animals found their way into the troops' tents with alarming frequency. During the year of 1872, sixteen men died of rabies after having been bitten by skunks.[162]

The treatment of alcoholics required a significant portion of the surgeon's time. The standard procedure was to confine the alcoholic to the hospital until he could be returned to his military duties. Although the official military position strongly condemned the habitual use of alcohol, the garrison was surprisingly forgiving of chronic offenders. Only those obviously incapable of continuing to soldier were discharged from the army.[163]

The combination of long rides or marches, unsuitable clothing and bitterly penetrating winters on the plains resulted in a high incidence of frostbite among the troops. Gangrene often set in before the men could be returned to the post for treatment. Most frostbite victims lost their affected limbs, as amputation was usually necessary to save the victim's life. Fortunately chloroform was usually available as an anesthetic before surgery; however, the men suffered considerably after the amputation had been completed.[164] Dr. Tremaine, who served Fort Dodge as a surgeon for ten years and performed several hundred amputations during his tour of duty, was quite vocal in his condemnation of the inadequate protection afforded troops on field duty during the winter months.[165] In the single year 1872 he removed frostbitten members from the persons of seventy men.[166]

Soldiers whose illness could not be diagnosed, who were insane or who required more delicate surgery than that performed at Fort Dodge were sent to various Eastern military hospitals for treatment.[167] Amputees, men who had been ruptured, chronic venereal cases, and those afflicted with the late stages of tuberculosis were usually discharged from the service.[168]

The casualties experienced during the scouts and marches, especially during years when the Indians were unusually hostile, compounded the task of the post hospital. The surgeon and his staff or orderlies had the added responsibility of caring for the sharply increased numbers of wounded in addition to the expected duties of treating the ill. Although additional surgeons and medical supplies were usually assigned to the fort prior to a major campaign, the modest medical resources of the post were invariably strained by the lengthened roll of wounded men.

This was especially so during the Sheridan Campaign of 1868-1869 and the Miles Campaign of 1874, when wounded civilians caught up in the struggle, as well as military casualties, were evacuated from the field and placed in the Fort Dodge hospital.[169] During the former expedition, which reached a climax in the midst of a severe winter, frostbite victims were admitted to the care of the post surgeon in greater numbers than battle casualties.[170]

The most common injuries sustained by soldiers in the field were concussions, incised wounds, arrow wounds, gun shot wounds and broken bones. Gangrene frequently infected open wounds because of the mediocre medical attention available in the field. The surgeons often chose to amputate injured limbs rather than risk the chance that gangrene would set in. As a result of such preventive surgery, a significant number of men who had received only minor wounds were unfortunately maimed for life.[171]

Cavalry troopers were especially susceptible to receiving broken bones. They were often thrown from horses in the field as a result of an animal's losing its footing or collapsing from exhaustion during sustained marches. Most frequently only legs or arms were shattered, but occasionally the neck or spine was broken by such falls; and if the unfortunate trooper survived, he was often permanently injured.[172] When detachments were in the field without the services of an accompanying surgeon, broken bones quite frequently were improperly set or perhaps went unattended altogether, thereby leaving the victims with a permanently twisted limb.

The wounds sustained during garrison duty were as often the result of fights as of injury received while detailed at work.[173] Suspected malingerers were at times treated rather roughly. Years of service had provided Dr. Tremaine with considerable insight into the motives of soldiers in his care, and he once completed surgery on the mangled hand of a man without administering an anesthetic, after his preliminary examination of the wound convinced him the trooper had intentionally blown off parts of two of his fingers so that he might be discharged from the service.[174]

In addition to their responsibility to the fort's military personnel, the post surgeons treated civilians from the surrounding area. Ranchers, buffalo hunters, railroad employees and members of wagon trains often sought medical attention at the post.[175] After Dodge City was established the residents of the cattle town frequently came to the fort for care until a doctor could be persuaded to establish a practice in the "wickedest little city on earth."[176]

Because they were usually the most highly educated members of the garrison, the surgeons were expected to keep a record of the weather by noting rainfall, storms and daily temperatures and to write a brief history of the post in the form of an annual report which was forwarded to the Office of the Surgeon General.[177] Dr. Tremaine established an excellent record with the army during his ten year tour of duty at Fort Dodge both as a medical officer and as an expert on military life. He was frequently called to Washington, D. C., where his advice was sought by Congressional committees.[178] The doctor carried on a personal crusade through the Office of the Surgeon General to relieve the frontier trooper of unusual and, in his opinion unnecessary, hardship. His petitions to Washington on behalf of the men he served, sought a more balanced diet, better post housing facilities, modern medical equipment, a serviceable system of sanitation and improved clothing for the task of frontier soldiering.[179]

In 1878, Dr. Tremaine's wife died of pneumonia. The bitterness of the personal loss noticeably blunted his ardor for military reform, and he resigned from the army shortly thereafter.[180] The soldiers of Fort Dodge, the citizens of Dodge City, and the farmers and ranchers of the surrounding community paid tribute to the surgeon as he prepared to leave the fort. He had delivered almost every child born in the area during his tour of duty. A significant number of the soldiers and cowboys who were present to extend their thanks to the doctor owed their lives to his skill at abstracting arrowheads and bullets.[181]

Honoring the Dead

The entire garrison was assembled in full dress uniform to attend the funerals of deceased soldiers. Six privates were regularly assigned as pallbearers, and an honor guard consisting of a corporal and eight privates always stood watch at the casket. The services were conducted according to paragraph eight hundred twenty-three of Upton's Infantry Tactics. Following the burial a full dress parade was held in honor of the dead.[182]

When President Garfield died from the effects of an assassin's bullet in 1881, the entire day of his burial was reserved for services. Thirteen guns were fired in the President's honor at dawn and a single gun was fired at thirty minute intervals throughout the remainder of the day. At the close of the day a thirty-eight gun salute was fired. Twenty-six days after the burial the final tribute, a twenty-one gun salute, was fired. No labor was permitted on the reservation during the entire course of the day. The flag was lowered to half mast, and a full dress parade was held at 10:00 A.M. The officers were ordered to wear a badge of mourning on their left arms and on their swords for six months after the burial.[183]

The personal effects of fallen officers and enlisted men were collected and sent to their families. However, if no relatives were listed on the records of the deceased, their material goods were auctioned off at the post.[184] Officers frequently owned the horses they rode, and the animals were shipped to the next of kin if the owner died while on duty at the fort.[185]

In addition to the soldiers who were buried at Fort Dodge, a number of civilians were interred at the post cemetery. These included deceased civilian employees, their wives and children, as well as the dead gathered by the troopers from Indian depredations.[186]

The relatives of deceased citizens from Dodge City often hesitated to bury their loved ones at the site provided by the town because of the former notoriety of many of the cemetery's occupants. Their requests to inter their dead at Fort Dodge were usually granted. Included on the cemetery roll was Edward Masterson, the brother of William "Bat" Masterson and the marshal of Dodge City before he was shot down by a drunken cowboy.[187] It was a common judgment about the raw little cowtown, that "the rich are buried at Fort Dodge, but the cowhands and the poor either rest on Boot Hill or have gone on to hell."

CHAPTER IV

THE CLIMAX OF RETRIBUTION: FORT DODGE AND THE PLAINS CAMPAIGNS, 1868-1875

The Aftermath of the Medicine Lodge Treaty

Throughout the winter of 1868 and the following spring a major contest took shape over the buffalo hunting grounds of western Kansas. The Peace Commission, which had recently structured the abortive Medicine Lodge Treaty, met at Chicago to continue deliberations on the thorny Indian problem;[1] but the final solution to the dilemma would rest with the military.

As a result of the transfer of the Plains hunting grounds at Medicine Lodge, the army anticipated pressing the Indians with a major offensive with perhaps less hindrance from those who preferred a more humane approach in the event hostilities were resumed. General Sherman plotted the military's course of action with little hesitation: "We have now selected and provided reservations for all off the great road. All who cling to their old hunting grounds are hostile and will remain so till killed off."[2] In fact, the general could not resist the opportunity to reduce the eventual outcome to a simple matter of subtraction. "The more we can kill this year," Sherman went on, "the less will have to be killed the next war, for the more I see of these Indians the more convinced I am that all have to be killed or maintained as a species of pauper. Their attempts at civilization are simply ridiculous."[3]

The Indians looked forward to another round of fighting with perhaps as much satisfaction as that radiating from the military. Medicine Lodge was remembered as the site of final humiliation where much of their most valued remaining possessions, the irreplaceable buffalo pastures north of the Arkansas River, had been taken from them in exchange for a scanty supply of government annuities.

During the winter months the southern tribes gathered near Fort Dodge and Fort Larned to claim their government rations and bide their time until warm weather returned. Their presence in western Kansas was an obvious breach of the Medicine Lodge Treaty, yet they were there at the invitation of their government agents to facilitate the distribution of annuities.[4] It should not have been too surprising that by May of 1868 they were once again roaming the plains north of the Arkansas, committed to their annual pattern of migration in the wake of the buffalo herds.

Throughout the course of the winter, minor incidents of hostility troubled the Fort Dodge garrison. Although no loss of life was recorded before the following spring, the disgruntled plainsmen kept active by stealing livestock until they were no longer dependent on the government for their food and clothing.[5] By mid-March the threat of deprivation had been removed, and they returned to the Cimarron to prey on passing trains.

An unprecedented era of growth had pushed the settler's frontier steadily westward in Kansas during the post-Civil War years. During 1867 alone, fifty thousand immigrants converged on the state intent on claiming the state's rich central prairies.[6] The rapid expansion of commercial farming necessarily foreshadowed the end of the classic Plains Indian culture. Hundreds of thousands of acres of prairie were broken out by the plow each year as the bison's feeding grounds were methodicaly converted to wheat and corn fields. Ironically the demise of the buffao herds preceded that of the prairie itself as the lumbering animals were preyed upon just for the sport of killing, or for the financial returns realized from the sale of hides or selected cuts of meat.

By late spring of 1868, a general assault was once again unleashed along the frontier by the southern tribes. As the casualties mounted, the frightened populace flocked to the safety of small towns, where they barricaded themselves against the atrocities befalling many of their friends who remained on their homesteads.[7] Crops and livetock were abandoned in the fields as their owners chose poverty over the risk of sudden death.

The governor's office was besieged with petitions for relief rations and militia protection. Irate citizens advised Governor Samuel Crawford to "make peace with the devils Chivington style."[8] One settler found that his community's threats of reprisals against the Indians were wearing thin:

> Governor Crafford Dear Sir
>
> by the request of meny of our sitisanry I wright yow the condisions of afairs in southwestern kansas and the deppedation commited on our settlers by the indians thay have kiled no one latley that we no of but air coming into our settlement in armed forse and drives of our property and air very sassy and impedent all that saves the murder of settlers is we keep thretning with yow but thay cam to the conclusion after awhile that there is no dainger that it is all a sceare[9]

By late summer the atrocities had become unbearable, and Kansas militia units were again gathered for punitive campaigns. Governor Crawford, obviously disappointed with the inability of federal troops to contain the attacks, appealed directly to the President:

> EXECUTIVE DEPARTMENT
> Topeka, August 22, 1868
>
> His Excellency Andrew Johnson, President of the United States, Washington, District of Columbia.
>
> The Indians are again committing depredations in Western Kansas.
>
> Last week they killed and wounded thirty men, women and children, ravished seven women and carried away one young lady — burned a number of houses and captured a large amount of stock and other property.

Frontier settlers were driven in some sixty miles, leaving everything at the mercy of these red-handed fiends.

Wounded women were ravished and otherwise most inhumanely treated in presence of their own dying husbands and children.

In the name of God and humanity must we submit to these atrocities, and see the Indians under the care and protection of the Government, go unpunished?

I appeal to you for protection, and respectfully, but earnestly request that you cause to be driven, at once, from this state, the Kiowas, Commanches, Arrapahoes, Apaches and Cheyenne Indians, perpetrators of the recent outrages and many others committed in Kansas during the past four years.

If the Government cannot protect its own citizens, let the fact be made known that the people may endeavor to protect themselves, or if volunteers are needed I will furnish the Government all that may be necessary to insure a permanent and lasting peace.

The Commission is a mockery and a disgrace to the nation. I trust therefore that you will keep the commissioners at home, and stop the issueing of arms, amunition and supplies to hostile Indians while they are robbing, murdering and outraging a defensless people.

S. J. Crawford
Governor of Kansas[10]

On August 23, General Sheridan decreed that all Indians met by the military within the borders of Kansas would be attacked and driven from the state as quickly as possible.[11] General Alfred Sully was ordered to gather troops at Fort Dodge for a punitive expedition southward into the Indian Territory. It was hoped that the threat posed by General Sully's movements would draw the warring bands back to their reservations to protect their women and children and thus relieve the frontier from the intense raiding endured through much of the summer.

Prior to General Sully's arrival, the Fort Dodge garrison had once again been hard pressed to hold the field in the face of the attacks meted out in the vicinity of the post. Although the trains moving along the Santa Fe Route bore the brunt of the assault, the fort's casualties from field engagements mounted steadily. One raid was made directly against the post, with four troopers being killed and seventeen wounded.[12]

No sooner had Sully crossed the Arkansas River than he was under continual harassment and engagement. Both the advance and rear guards of his command were kept close to the main body of troops by the menacing charges of shadowing bands of warriors. Several forays against the supply van and the expedition's cavalry herd netted the attackers a considerable number of horses and mules.[13]

Between September 11 and 15 the command fought several minor battles, and on the latter date the troops were drawn into an ambush where both sides sustained heavy losses. Intelligence reports gathered by Sully's scouts indicated that the Indians were massing for a major assault, and the general quickly lost courage and retraced his line of march back to Fort Dodge.[14] The retreat proved even more difficult than the move southward, and the command reached the safety of the post only after perhaps averting a major defeat had they chosen to continue to contest the field with the southern tribes.

A second column operating to the north under the command of Major George A. Forsyth was less fortunate. General Sheridan had ordered the major to collect fifty civilian scouts from the Fort Hays area in late August to police the field along the Smoky Hill Route.[15] The recruitment of the scouts was considered necessary because of the inadequate number of veteran cavalry troops available within the Department of the Missouri. As the unit moved westward from Fort Wallace in early September, they discovered the trail left by the travois of a small band of Cheyennes. The trail grew more distinct as the initial party was joined by several hundred fellow Cheyennes; yet Major Forsyth, against the advice of several of the more experienced scouts, determined to continue the pursuit.[16]

On the night of September 16 the scouts camped on a small island approximately forty yards long and one hundred yards wide in the midst of the Arickaree River, just across the Colorado boundary. The small island afforded the only protection available on the rolling prairies of this section of the high plains.

At dawn the men were awakened by the war cries of several hundred Cheyennes. A furious contest ensued. Major Forsyth was immediately struck by three bullets, yet he remained conscious and continued to guide the course of the battle for the island.[17] The unit's surgeon, Dr. Mooers, and the officer second in command, Lieutenant Beecher, as well as several enlisted men, were mortally wounded before the men could excavate pits in the island's sand.[18] Both the scouts and the Cheyennes entrenched themselves, and a four day exchange of gunfire ensued. Four of the scouts volunteered to attempt to bring relief and slipped out, two on the first night and two on the second, and ran and walked toward Fort Wallace, which lay one hundred and twenty-five miles to the east. The Cheyennes broke off the attack on the fifth day, but the scouts were forced to remain on the island in the midst of the stench of dead horses and without food as they feared being caught in the open if the Indians returned to continue the engagement.

On the ninth day a detachment of the U. S. Tenth Cavalry reached the beleagured scouts. Five were found dead and eighteen were wounded, while the entire unit was suffering from hunger and exposure.[19]

At about the same time a wagon guard of four enlisted men from Fort Dodge, which had been sent to Fort Larned to secure the post's mail, was struck by a large war party near Little Coon Creek. The men hastily threw up a barricade by utilizing the wagon and several dead horses. As the battle continued three of the men were seriously wounded. The attackers repeatedly sent waves of horsemen against the stronghold, but the little group continued to hold out until nightfall.

As darkness set in the only man not wounded, Corporal Patrick O'Boyle of the Seventh Cavalry, volunteered to take the remaining horse and ride to Fort Dodge for help. On his departure he threw his weapons to his fellow troopers with the advice: "Here boys, you want them more than I do."[20] After a hard ride during which the corporal was pursued by four braves to within a mile of the post, help was quickly gathered, and the wounded men were relieved from attack.

Private James Goodwin had received a gun shot wound in the shoulder, Private John O'Donnell had suffered bullet wounds in the thigh, neck and face, and Private Charles Faton had wounds in one arm and his buttocks.[21]

Lord Frederick Haxby, a visiting Englishman who happened to be at the post when the men were brought in, lionized their stand through articles sent to several Eastern newspapers and by hastily writing a short ballad called "The Battle of Little Coon Creek."

THE BALLAD OF LITTLE COON CREEK

SONG

Calm and bright shone the sun on the morning
 That four men from Fort Dodge marched away,
With food and supplies for their comrades —
 They were to reach Big Coon Creek that day;
'Tis a day we shall all well remember,
 That gallant and brave little fight,
How they struggled and won it so bravely —
 Though wounded, still fought through the night.

CHORUS

So let's give three cheers for our comrades,
 That gallant and brave little band,
Who, against odds, would never surrender.
 But bravely by their arms did they stand.

Fifty Indians surprised them while marching,
 Their scalps tried to get, but in vain;
The boys repulsed them at every endeavor,
 They were men who were up to their game.
"Though the red-skins are ten times our number,.
 We coolly on each other rely,"
Said the Corporal in charge of the party,
 "We'll conquer the foe or we'll die!"

Still they fought with a wit and precision;
Assistance at last came to hand
Two scouts on the action appearing
To strengthen the weak little band.
Then one charged right clear through the Indians,
To Fort Dodge for help he did go,
While the balance still kept up the fighting,
And gallantly beat off the foe.

A squadron of cavalry soon mounted,
Their comrades to rescue and save.
General Sully, he issued an order,
Applauding their conduct so brave.
And when from their wounds they recovered,
Many years may they live to relate,
The fight that occurred in September,
In the year eighteen sixty-eight.[22]

Not too surprisingly the courage of the men proved more enduring than the ballad. All four were eventually awarded the Congressional Medal of Honor.

The Road to the Washita

On October 9 General Sheridan was given authority by the Department of War to commence preparations for a winter campaign into the Indian Territory.[23] The advocates of pacification in dealing with the southern tribes had first been placed on the defensive and then silenced almost altogether by the ferocity of the assault on the Kansas frontier. Several of the government agents assigned to the plains reluctantly admitted the necessity of chastising the guilty bands if order was to be restored.[24]

By early fall the focal point of the raids centered along the Santa Fe Trail as the warring redmen commenced a slow migration southward toward their families and their winter camp grounds. The forthcoming campaign was designed to pursue the offending Indians and to attack them soon after they had gathered at their southern homes.[25]

General Sheridan's field strategy pivoted on the assembly of three punitive columns that would close on the Indians from the north, west and south, thereby blocking all avenues of escape and forcing the tribes to stand and fight. The primary force was to be gathered at Fort Dodge under the personal supervision of General Sully, who was instructed to ready eleven companies of the U. S. Seventh Cavalry, three companies of the U. S. Third Infantry and one company of the U. S. Thirty-Eighth Infantry for the march.[26]

As soon as the troops were ready to take the field, the general was to move southward and establish a secondary depot which was later named Camp Supply. Four hundred thousand rations were deposited at Fort Dodge to be moved to the new depot as they were needed.[27] Here the command was to be complemented by the addition of the 19th Kansas Voluntary Cavalry Regiment consisting of twelve companies of men.[28] After this juncture, the column was to continue the march southward toward the anticipated Indian encampments along either the Washita or Red Rivers.

The flight of the Indians to the south was to be contained by a detachment of eight companies of troops from Fort Bascom, New Mexico Territory, and to the west by a second unit of five companies sent out from Fort Lyon. These forces were to act as "beaters," driving the Indians toward the main force proceeding southward.[29]

The March of the 19th Kansas Cavalry

General Sheridan arrived at Camp Supply on November 21, to supervise the campaign personally. He noted:

> I deemed it best to go in person as the campaign was an experimental one — campaigns at such a season having been deemed impracticable and reckless by old and experienced frontiersmen, and I did not like to expose the troops to great hazard, without being present myself to judge of their hardships and privations.[30]

On his arrival at the base of supply, the general was disappointed to find that the Kansas troops had not yet arrived. The regiment had left Topeka, Kansas, on November 5, in good spirits. Governor Crawford had resigned his office to take personal command of the unit. The men were dressed in new uniforms, mounted on excellent horses; and as the crowd that had assembled to see them off cheered energetically they vowed to settle the issue at stake by thoroughly chastising the treacherous "red-skins."[31]

The heady exuberance of the parade was soon forgotten as the regiment moved into the field. Cold rain and drizzle set in, and the men carried only nine days' rations for themselves and their horses. Within the first week of the campaign desertions were already heavy.[32] The line of march followed by the command was southward from Topeka until the troops reached the small town of Wichita. Here they turned westward, intending to rendezvous with General Sheridan at Camp Supply.

All went well until the cavalrymen reached the Cimarron Canyons, still several days' march from Camp Supply. While they were wandering among the ravines attempting to decide in which direction to proceed, a severe blizzard set in, and the troops were snowbound for almost two weeks. Although the men were able to subsist rather comfortably on fresh buffalo meat, the horses died in droves from lack of food and water and from exposure.[33]

On November 23, scouts sent out from Camp Supply discovered the Kansas regiments, who were eventually brought into Camp Supply, minus seven hundred of their mounts.[34] Shortly after their arrival a bitter argument ensued as to who should bear the blame for the debacle in the Cimarron Canyons. The officers claimed that the chief of scouts, William "Apache Bill" Seaman, had led the unit astray, while he was equally insistent that the novice cavalrymen had chosen to disregard his advice while seeking a short cut to Camp Supply. Although the issue was never satisfactorily settled, largely because few could agree where the unit had been and exactly who had been setting the line of march, "Apache Bill" was dismissed and sent back to Fort Dodge.[35]

Custer at the Washita

Ironically the embarrassing stay in the canyons had undoubtedly prevented the 19th Kansas Cavalry from sharing General Custer's impending mantle as the perpetrator of a massacre. Sheridan had decided to commence the winter offensive without the Kansas troops and had ordered Custer to take the field on November 23, the same day the wanderers had been located in the canyons.[36]

Custer had been recalled from his year's suspension just as the troops were being readied at Fort Dodge in early November.[37] On his arrival at Camp Supply, he had immediately quarreled with Sully over the plans then being finalized for attacking the Indians. Sheridan recognized the incompatibility of the two officers and, undoubtedly influenced by the cautious conservatism demonstrated the past summer when Sully's command had been driven back to the protection of Fort Dodge, placed Custer in command of field operations and relegated his opponent to the secondary position of bringing up supply trains from Fort Dodge.[38]

On November 26, Custer struck the trail of a band of Cheyennes and Arapahoes that had been harassing the scouts, messengers and supply trains along the road between Fort Dodge and Camp Supply.[39] Several men had been shot from the saddle and scalped by this party during the early weeks of the campaign. By late November the task of carrying correspondence had become so hazardous that cash bounties would no longer attract scouts, and volunteers had been called for from among Sheridan's corps of officers.[40]

Once the trail was found Custer, having been led to Chief Black Kettle's encampment on the Washita, pursued the raiding party tenaciously, and on the following morning history repeated itself. In much the same way that Colonel Chivington had ridden down on Black Kettle's band at Sand Creek, the general's dawn assault caught his quarry completely by surprise, and one hundred and three Indians fell before the cavalry charge. General Custer lost two officers and twenty enlisted men, while three officers and eleven enlisted men were wounded.[41]

As the initial confusion of battle subsided, ominous gatherings of warriors were sighted from nearby undetected Indian encampments. Their presence persuaded the general that he should retreat from the field as quickly as possible. He gathered fifty-three prisoners, all of whom were women and children, shot several hundred captured ponies and, after burning the village, abruptly withdrew to Camp Supply.[42]

During the return march the captive women were shared by the troops.[43] General Custer himself reserved several of the squaws to personally attend his tent.[44] From Camp Supply the women and children were sent back to Fort

Dodge, where the surgeons noted that many of the captives were in need of immediate medical attention as a result of their stay with men of the Seventh Cavalry.[45]

The Policy of Intimidation

The sudden onslaught of retribution visited on the Cheyennes by Custer satisfied Sheridan that for the present time no further hostile raids need be anticipated. Sheridan held little compassion for the lot of the Indians. The demise of Black Kettle, a man who in his words was "a worn out and worthless old cypher," and his band were considered to be a just but inadequate measure of compensation for the settlers and soldiers who had lost their lives along the frontier.[46]

On December 7 the command took the field again, this time with the 19th Kansas Cavalry added to the Seventh Cavalry. The Kansas contingent was of dubious value as they trudged along on foot after having lost most of their mounts in the Cimarron Canyons. The sudden annihilation of Black Kettle's people had panicked several other Cheyenne, Arapahoe and Kiowa bands in the vicinity. A number had moved eastward, further into the Indian Territory, while others, convinced that no salvation other than flight remained for them, pushed westward to the extremity of the Indian Territory or on into the Texas Panhandle.

Sheridan retraced the steps of the Seventh Cavalry back to the scene of the struggle on the Washita, where he reclaimed the bodies of eighteen of General Custer's men who had been left on the field as they had fallen. Here the trail of a second body of Indians moving down the river was discovered. Several days later the campaigners caught the surprised Indians encamped along the Washita. Unlike the other tribes who had previously moved to safer quarters, the Kiowas had been convinced that no further campaigning was possible due to the harshness of winter and had remained near the scene of Custer's attack.[47]

Before the troops could be assembled for a second engagement along the Washita, several of the Kiowas approached the command with a letter from their agent, General W. B. Hazen, which advised Sheridan that he had extended amnesty to his charges.[48] That night under the cover of darkness all of the Kiowas escaped and fled toward the safety of the Wichita Mountains, except for twenty of the leading men, who remained to council with Sheridan. This act so infuriated the general that he ordered Chiefs Satanta and Lone Wolf arrested and hanged if the Kiowas did not return. This threat proved most effective, and within a few days the Kiowas had been assembled for winter confinement on their reservation. Sheridan later admitted that Hazen's refusal to allow the troops to attack the Kiowas had been most disappointing. Even more irritating perhaps was the escape from the hangman's noose of Satanta and Lone Wolf. "I shall always regret that I did not hang those Indians," the general mused later, "and I shall always regret that I did not punish the whole tribe when I first met them."[49]

The stand off with the Kiowas dulled Sheridan's thirst for winter campaigning and, after directing General Custer to remain in the field to search out any remaining bands still off their reservations, the general retired from the field.[50] Custer later discovered an encampment of Cheyennes and Arapahoes on the headwaters of the Red River, which he coerced into releasing two white women held captive by threatening to hang six of their chiefs and warriors.[51]

On April 7, the campaigners reached Fort Hays, where the Seventh Cavalry went into quarters and the 19th Kansas Cavalry was mustered out. Sheridan was not on hand to greet the troops. On his return from the field he had been met by a courier who brought him the message that General Grant had been inaugurated President. Sherman had been chosen to fill the general's place as Commanding General of the Army, and he had been promoted to command the Division of the Missouri.[52] In his later report to Sherman he noted:

> I am now able to report that there has been a fulfillment of all the conditions which we had in view when we commenced our winter's campaign; punishment was inflicted; property destroyed and the Indians disabused of the idea that winter would bring security.[53]

President Grant and the Quakers

True to the form of past experience, the bloodshed at the Washita directed a new round of condemnation of military policy toward the plains tribes. President Grant's stay at the White House had tended to isolate him from the realities of Indian warfare, and he was obviously becoming more responsive to the pleas of Eastern humanitarians for a major overhauling of the government's traditional stance.[54]

The average agent representing the plains tribes was admitted to be mediocre by both the army and the Indian Bureau. More often than not the more attractive positions were given to political faithfuls, while the less lucrative posts were manned by itinerant "frontiersmen" who immediately set about lining their own pockets at the expense of their native subjects.[55]

The President's first appointment after the announcement during the spring of 1869 of his intentions to reform the bureau was that of Ely S. Parker, a former Seneca agent and a man who had stood beside his benefactor at the siege of Vicksburg, to the office of Commissioner of Indian Affairs.[56] Although it was anticipated that the ranks of the new cadre of agents would be filled by the devout of several religious denominations, it was most often a member of the Society of Friends that stepped forward to offer his services; hence the labeling of the program the "Quaker Policy."'

Commissioner Parker and his eventual successor, Francis J. Walker, both recognized that the heart of the confusion relative to the status of the Indians lay in the government's long standing position that the tribes legally remained individual ethnic entities and must therefore be dealt with as subjects of foreign nations. Commission Walker offered the criticism that:

> The failure of the Congress, for a period of more than eighty years after the adoption of the constitution and for forty years after the epochal decision in *Cherokee Nation vs Georgia,* to provide a more appropriate method of regulating the relation of Indian tribes to the federal government, like the failure during more than a century and a half to define the term "Indian," affords a striking illustration of the indefinite and haphazard manner in which Indian affairs have been conducted. Obviously, the exact legal relationship of Indian tribes to the federal government should have been determined at one of the earliest sessions of Congress, and just as obviously, with hundreds of laws being enacted and hundreds of millions of dollars being appropriated for the benefit of a special class of inhabitants, a definition of the individuals who should form such a class should have been established by Congressional authority long before the present time.[57]

Although for several years, between 1869 and 1874, the frequency of Indian depredations on the southern plains diminished sharply, it is difficult to weigh and assess the relative merit of several factors involved in bringing about this reduction. Without doubt the blow at the Washita did much to persuade the southern tribes that further resistance was suicidal. For the first time punitive warfare had been visited on their people within the confines of their assigned reservation homes, thereby graphically demonstrating the capacity of the army to seek out and attack their quarry while leaving no sanctuary of safety available.

The expanding of the settler's and transportation frontiers undoubtedly served to reduce the number of Indian attacks. It was no longer possible for stealthy raiding parties to appear without previous detection and to assault startled settlers or railroad hands before the military was aware of their presence. The paths of war parties who rode north of the Arkansas River in violation of the Medicine Lodge agreement were immediately reported by ranchers or residents of small towns, and troops were quickly dispatched to the scene, often by rail cars, to intercept the marauders. The friendly open prairie into which these bands had formerly melted was now a sea of hostility that promised sudden retribution to those who violated the sanctity of advancing civilization.

As an addition to the protection from violence provided by the frontier and the army, the Quaker policy undoubtedly lessened the friction between red men and white. A genuine attempt was made to alter the cultural patterns of the plains dwellers by demonstrating the benefits that might accrue to those who forsook the ways of the plains journeyman for the more confining life of the agrarian. At first glance the accomplishments of the Friends appear to have been quite modest; however, the question remains as to whether a fair trial was or could be given to the program within the hostile setting of the plains.

The ignorance and scars of the past persuaded the frontier Kansan that the ultimate solution had not changed:

> The government has sent out a few civil Quakers to deal with these

treacherous savages. With as much propriety might they cast a lamb among the wolves. Even Penn could not palliate the cruel deeds of hostile Indians of today. Many plans have been tried to produce peace on the border; but one alternative remains — EXTERMINATION.[58]

The Day of the Buffalo Hunter

Ironically it was not the threat of personal extermination, rather the rapid demise of their "staff of life," the plains bison, that initiated a final outburst of warfare on the plains. In 1871 a young Vermont wood-cutter, John Mooar, who was working at Fort Hays, supplied raw buffalo hides to an eastern firm, who immediately devised a successful technique for tanning the skins, thereby producing a superior quality leather.[59] Prior to this discovery the hides had been sold with the hair still intact as robes or souvenirs, provided in limited quantities by the Indians themselves.

Mooar's discovery created an immediate market for the hides at three dollars and fifty cents each.[60] The Atchison, Topeka and Santa Fe Railroad reached Fort Dodge and its frontier sibling, Dodge City, in 1872, and dozens of hunters, restless to claim the returns from the anticipated slaughter, gathered at the end of the track.[61] In addition to the saloons and general stores of Dodge City, hide purchasing businesses immediately sprang up, and the soiled little town soon became the center of the great buffalo hunt.

A majority of the hides taken eventually proved to be worthless because of the damage inflicted by novice skinners. Even with this great loss to ineptness the market was soon glutted, and the value of prime hides shrank to one dollar in 1873.[62] In the space of only two years the buffalo in the grazing herds north of the Arkansas River were completely annihilated.

Several million head had fallen before the tenacious hunters and their Sharps Fifty rifles. By 1874, they were looking southward across the river to the last remnants of the southern herd. These animals provided the southern tribes with the bulk of their food. Only a spark was needed to renew Indian hostilities on the plains.

The Siege of Adobe Walls

During the fall of 1873, a group of buffalo hunters, anticipating the necessity of moving their operations south of the Arkansas the next spring, visited the commander at Fort Dodge. Colonel Richard I. Dodge had returned to the post for a second tour of duty. The hunters rather cautiously attempted to secure from the colonel some indication of the army's expected response to their entering the last southern reserve of the buffalo. Colonel Dodge had for some time emphatically supported General Sheridan's and General Sherman's contention that the plains tribes could only be subdued if the herds were completely destroyed, thereby forcing the Indians to rely entirely on the government for provisions.[63] The red man would undoubtedly not leave their reservations if the empty plains, devoid of the last herds of bison, promised nothing more attractive than slow starvation.

The colonel realized that new hostilities could be expected if the hunters violated the territory south of the river, and he was equally aware that he had no authority to initiate the slaughter of the bison. This delicate problem was handled by the officer's thinly veiled suggestion: "Boys if I were a buffalo hunter, I would hunt where the buffalo are."[64]

The tacit suggestion that the army would probably not interfere with the hunter's plans was all that was needed. The following spring a group of enterprising Dodge City merchants struck out for the Texas Panhandle. Their numbers included Tom O'Keefe, a blacksmith; A. C. Meyers, a merchant; Jim Hanrahan, a saloon keeper; and William Olds and his wife, who hoped to open a restaurant.[65] They anticipated draining off as much of the financial returns to be realized from the venture as possible by selling their merchandise and services to the free spending hunters, as well as having first choice on the hides taken before the remainder were freighted back to Dodge City for sale and shipment to the east. The list of prospective hide buyers included Charles Rath and Robert Wright. Rath had previously infuriated military authorities by his sale of large quantities of firearms and powder to the Kiowas, while his partner, Wright, had found the military equally unwilling to tolerate his practice of "indiscriminate" distribution of whiskey.[66]

All went as expected within the newly established little adobe community until late in the spring. At this juncture a band of Kwahadi Comanches, infuriated by recent losses sustained during a sortie against the supposedly docile Tonkawas, undertook to recoup their lost prestige at the expense of the inhabitants of Adobe Walls.[67] Although there was considerable hesitation by a major portion of the party to attack whites again, their confidence of success was buoyed by the promises of a newly emerging medicine man. Isatai announced to his tribesmen that he could disgorge rifle cartridges in prolific quantities from his stomach and that he possessed a "paint" that would render them impervious to the bullets of the buffalo hunters.[68]

A beaten and discouraged people were perhaps willing to gamble on such dubious promises of mystic power even though past experiences with shaman had proved disappointing. The Kwahadi Chief, Quanah Parker, a half-breed born of Cynthia Ann Parker, a captive white woman and a Comanche brave, gathered his warriors along with a number of adventurous Kiowas and Cheyennes and set out for the hunters' settlement.[69]

News of the impending attack was carried to Adobe Walls by several disgruntled Comanches who had refused to believe in the spiritual capacities of Isatai; however, only the merchants were forewarned that the assault would occur on June 27, and they chose to keep this information from the hunters, who remained busily engaged at the task of killing and skinning.[70] The merchants were persuaded that if they shared the warning, the hunters might strike out for Dodge City, thereby forcing their business-conscious partners to do the same or risk the consequences of attack.

As the day of the forecast raid approached, the merchants and buyers lost their nerve, and all but Hanrahan and O'Keefe rode for Dodge City.[71] Their flight placed the saloon keeper and the blacksmith in a difficult position. Should they warn the hunters, the embarrassing question of the source of their knowledge might well be asked. If they remained silent, they could well be massacred along with the unsuspecting buffalo men.

Hanrahan handled this prickly problem with unusual candor. At approximately three o'clock in the morning he fired a pistol shot and then told a number of inquisitive hunters that one of the saloon's primary beams was cracking. After a supporting timber had been placed under the supposedly weakening roof and Hanrahan had demonstrated his gratitude by providing free drinks, several of the hunters decided to prepare for another day of killing buffaloes.[72] As they strode outdoors into the first light of dawn a line of approaching Comanches was discovered, and almost immediately the battle was joined. During the first hectic moments the Indians came perilously close to overrunning the buildings, but after the shock of the first assault was contained, the opposing belligerents settled down to a sustained sniping contest.[73]

As quickly as possible a messenger was sent for help, but his reception at Fort Dodge several days later was less than cordial.[74] It had become apparent before the runner from Adobe Walls arrived that a serious uprising was rapidly taking shape, but the source of the Indian's displeasure was still not known. The unlawful entry of the hunters into the grounds south of the Arkansas had not been detected by the new post commander, Major Charles E. Compton, who had replaced Colonel Dodge after he had already advised the buffalo men to "go where the buffalo are."[75]

The major immediately advised General John Pope, who had succeeded General Sheridan as commander of the Department of the Missouri, of the siege of the hunters and asked for further orders. The general, infuriated that the greed of a few men had unleashed another bath of bloodshed along the frontier, replied with a scathing telegram asking the major to "inform me at once by telegraph for what purpose and by what authority and where have these trading posts been established near the Canadian River."[76]

In his haste to secure relief the messenger from Adobe Walls had distorted the real purpose of the men still there. He pleaded that they had only established a trading post to "secure buffalo robes from the Indians."[77] Although no mention was made of the slaughter being carried on against the remnant of the last southern herd, Pope soon learned the truth, and for several days it appeared that he would refuse to send troops to the aid of the beleaguered men.

Charles Rath and Bob Wright, by now suffering from conscience pangs as a result of their having abandoned the men to an uncertain fate at the hand of the Indians, petitioned Governor Thomas A. Osborn to intercede with Pope.[78] The general first replied that he "would not send troops to protect unlawful trading posts south of Fort Dodge when he needed his troops to protect the Kansas frontier"; however, he later grudgingly relented, and a detachment was dispatched from Fort Dodge to relieve the hunters.[79]

Of the twenty-seven men and one woman who had been attacked at Adobe Walls, three men had been killed. The Indians, in spite of Isatai's powerful medicine, lost thirteen dead and a great many more wounded. The disgruntled hunters, their hope of a lucrative season of killing buffalo having vanished, placed the heads of the fallen Comanches on stakes, packed up their gear and headed back for Dodge City.[80] Their battle was over, but the task of the military in subduing the aroused Indians in the wake of yet another breach of good faith in guaranteeing their last hunting ground was just beginning.

"Hold the Line of the Arkansas"

Although the presence of a considerable body of buffalo hunters at Adobe Walls served as the immediate cause of the hostilities, it was not only this single breach of good faith, rather the swift and methodical slaughter of all the buffalo in the southern herd that prodded the Indians to stand and fight once more. The reliability of annuity deliveries still left much to be desired, and the southern tribes had frequently spent much of the winter deprived of the supplies essential to their continued existence. When promised assistance failed to materialize, the warriors could usually trust the buffalo to provide needed food. However, if they stood by without contesting the annihilation of the huge beasts, they would have no alternative for the future other than complete submission to the will of the goverment.

The Department of the Missouri was well aware of the growing probability of renewed bloodshed throughout the summer and fall of 1873. Intelligence reports indicated that dissatisfaction among plains tribes was increasing rapidly and the cause of their unrest was often bluntly stated, as was the following correspondence returned by an officer from Fort Dodge who had witnessed firsthand the Indian's response to the depletion of the buffalo herds:

> From Medicine Lodge and Wescaluga Creek east to the head of Beaver Creek on the west the country is filled with parties of from three to twelve buffalo hunters encamped for hunting on Clear Creek, a tributary of Beaver Creek, about thirty miles inside of the line of the Indian Territory and within the Cheyenne and Arapahoe Reservation.
>
> Two or three parties of buffalo hunters soon after made their camps on Clear Creek, one within a mile of Whirlwind's camp. They soon killed, or drove off all the buffalo and the Indians had to move their camp to another locality, from which it is very probable they will soon be driven as before.
>
> The Indians kill buffalo slowly, as they can cure the meat and skins, the hunters kill all they can at a time and skin afterwards. The Indians cannot compete with these hunters, and if some steps are not at once taken to stop these hunters, one of two things must occur. Either the Indians becoming exasperated will drive out the hunters, probably with bloodshed—which will inaugurate a war, or they will fail to obtain their winter's supply of meat and skins, which means their starvation or extreme suffering.

> I warned all the hunters out of the Indian Territory and off the Reservations. They move their camps back north to the state line of Kansas, or south to the state line of Texas, and from thence hunt in the Indian Territory and reservations as before. I may arrest trespassers in the Territory or Reservation, but must release them as soon as I reach the State line, there being no law to prevent them hunting either in Kansas or Texas.
>
> In my opinion very serious consequences will result unless immediate steps are taken to arrest the work of these hunters in the Indian Territory and Reservations.[81]

A rash of sorties were unleashed along the line of the Arkansas River in the wake of the struggle at Adobe Walls. The completion of the railroad to Dodge City had sharply reduced the volume of trade carried by wagon trains along the Santa Fe Route; however, those involved in shuttling goods by wagon along the dry route to Santa Fe, which was still without rail service, were forced to suspend operations or risk assault at the hands of several determined war parties.[82]

As soon as the report of the siege of the buffalo hunters had been received, troops from Fort Dodge were dispersed to take up positions along the river where they awaited the coming of the raiders.[83] Although strenuous efforts were made to hold the line from Sargent, Colorado Territory, to Wichita, Kansas, the task proved insurmountable for the thinly arrayed forces, and river crossings were effected at several points during the first week of July.[84] Once the Indians had gained access to the southern communities of settlers, a blood bath erupted. Farmers, ranchers, and railroad workmen bore the brunt of the assault. One surveying crew for the Atchison, Topeka and Santa Fe Railroad was caught without weapons, and six of the men forfeited their scalps in return for the error.[85] Twenty-two deaths were reported during the first month of hostilities.[86] Many panic-stricken agrarians fled to nearby towns to await their fates, while others who had had enough of frontier farming packed up and left for less dangerous parts. At the small community of Pierceville, some forty miles west of Fort Dodge, the Indians burned bridges and houses and threatened to wipe out the entire populace.[87]

As is often the case in war, the innocent suffered more than the guilty. The buffalo men, who had become the hunted rather than the hunters, scurried for the safety of Fort Dodge and several towns near the river, while less mobile citizens bore the brunt of the wave of atrocities. Ironically, five men were killed and scalped when attacked while delivering several wagon loads of annuities within the Indian Territory.[88]

Governor Osborn appealed directly to President Grant for troops to protect Kansas and for arms to distribute to militia and besieged settlements, but his efforts proved fruitless. The President, undoubtedly well informed as to the mediocre past performance of Kansas citizen soldiers and the grave responsibilities incurred by delivering arms to irate farmers, demurred. The President tersely replied that federal troops would provide all the protection needed in Kansas.[89]

Throughout the months of July and August the harried garrison at Fort Dodge searched the plains for marauding red men. Several pitched engagements were fought, but the menacing raiders could not be forced to retreat to their reservations. Only four companies of troops were available, two each of infantry and cavalry, and their ranks were quickly depleted by the extensive guard duties assigned to the garrison. General Pope prodded the officers to "pitch in to any party you can," but this was more easily asked for than accomplished.[90] The numerous calls for assistance along the line of the Arkansas could not be answered unless the troops were split into small detachments. Even at that only the more serious attacks could be dealt with.

Lesser incidents of violence went unchallenged as the reservoir of men available for field assignment was completely exhausted. One exasperated officer, hard pressed to explain the relative ineffectiveness of his detachment in the field, and apparently with a better grasp of prose composition than plains soldiering, pleaded the difficulty of "attempting to engage bloodthirsty bands of Indians." He noted they "flit about in small parties, here today and there tomorrow, seizing their prey in a moment, doing their hellish work, and off before help is at hand. Their trail is as difficult to trace as the orbit of a comet."[91]

No concerted attempt to punish the Indians could be considered until at least two or three companies had been gathered. The command was thus far unwilling to gamble on the success of such a venture until the embattled settlements along the frontier had first been secured.

Several emboldened war parties attacked railroad trains as they labored toward Dodge City. It was not unusual for the "ironhorses" to arrive pock marked with bullet holes and prickling with protruding arrows. Wild-eyed passengers, most of whom had just seen their first Indians and at that during one of their less attractive moments, cursed the railroads for exposing paying customers to the hazards of plains warfare. The railroad in turn successfully petitioned the military for armed guards to accompany each run along the route from Topeka to Dodge City.[92]

As fall approached and the raiders started their annual migration southward toward their reservations, the pressure on the Kansas frontier subsided. By September hostilities were largely confined to the vicinity between Fort Dodge and Camp Supply, and public attention focused on the anticipated winter campaign between the Washita and Red Rivers.

A Last Chastisement: General Miles at the Red River

With the resumption of fighting which had again broken out during the summer of 1874, the army methodically prepared for a re-enactment of the moderately successful Sheridan Campaign of 1868. Once again the primary force was assembled at Fort Dodge, but the "beater" columns were increased from two to four, and their points of departure for the field included Fort Griffin and Fort Concho, both within northern Texas, as well as Fort Lyon and Fort Union. The five divisions totaled some three thousand men as they left their respective garrisons.[93]

On the twenty-first of July General Nelson A. Miles was ordered to march southward to initiate again the encirclement of the reservations of warring bands. The general, still concerned that adequate supplies had not been gathered at Fort Dodge, waited until August 11 to move his troops.[94] Huge deposits of stores were in the process of being delivered by rail to depots on the Fort Dodge reservation in anticipation of several months of campaigning, and wagon masters were being contracted to move the supplies southward to support the command.

General Miles' initial thrust was disappointing in the immediate results that were realized. It was hoped that once he entered the field, thereby menacing those portions of the southern tribes not actively engaged in raiding, the war parties would hasten southward to protect their families and thus relieve the frontier from continued assault. Instead, the slowly returning warriors fell in behind the general's command and commenced intense assaults on his supply lines.[95] The general had so depleted the garrison at Fort Dodge in preparing his command that only a skeleton force had been left to maintain the post, and what cavalry troops remained were critically needed north of the river to engage lingering bands of hostiles.

With Fort Dodge incapable of providing adequate guards for trains and with the general unwilling to weaken his own position by splitting his column to provide protection, the sorties continued unabated and largely uncontested through much of the fall and winter. Ironically the casualties sustained at the general's rear often exceeded those incurred at the "front."[96]

After having reached the Washita, the main column moved westward onto the Staked Plains of the Texas Panhandle, fighting several brisk but minor engagements along the way with war parties bent on denying General Miles his invaluable supply van. The Staked Plain, a heavily undulated stretch of arid prairies bordering the mountain foothills to the west, was the home of the Kwahadi Comanches. Several bands of Cheyennes and Kiowas had fled to this area before the advance of the campaigners, undoubtedly fearing another assault such as that administered in 1868 by Custer at the Washita.

At Palo Duro Canyon, just above the Prairie Dog Fork of the Red River, the detachment of U. S. Fourth Cavalry from Fort Concho, Texas, under the command of Colonel Ranald Mackenzie, surprised four hundred fifty Cheyennes, Comanches and Kiowas. Although neither side suffered extensive casualties, the Indians' camp was captured, and all their supplies and ponies were destroyed by the advancing unit.[97]

Throughout the course of the winter, the army relentlessly pressed the bands, denying them respite and thereby steadily eroding the Indian's desire to continue resistance. Fourteen engagements were fought during the course of the winter, but in the end it was the tenacity of the army rather than losses in combat that broke the spirit of the red men.

As General Miles' troops pursued their quarry across the Staked Plains, the Fort Dodge garrison labored manfully to bring needed equipment and stores to the field. The winter of 1874 proved to be unusually severe, and by late November it was necessary to provide tents, heavier clothing and stoves for the shivering campaigners.[98] The efforts of the post to answer the frequent calls for supplies was seriously hampered by three severe blizzards that struck the plains during the course of the winter. Officers from Fort Dodge combed the frontier enlisting the help of farmers and ranchers, whose teams and wagons were sorely needed to expedite the transfer of goods.[99]

Contracts were issued on a transfer-of-weight basis. The firm of Otero Sellers and Company of eastern Colorado alone furnished the transportation for 800,000 pounds of supplies to be delivered at the front.[100] The teams and wagon masters suffered considerably during the course of the winter. Several men froze to death, while others burned the supplies and the wagons carrying them to escape the penetrating cold. During early January the temperature dipped to twenty-four degrees below zero, and for three weeks of that month the average temperature was only two degrees.[101]

Even during this extended period of intense cold, huge amounts of grains and stores were brought southward. By mid-February in excess of two million pounds of freight had been tediously hauled over the frozen plains.[102] In spite of the most strenuous efforts, General Miles continually prodded the garrison to speed the process of conveyance and delivery. Court-martial threats hung over the heads of officers responsible for late supplies, yet the picture of men suffering grievously from lack of foodstuffs and equipment that was sent back from the Staked Plains was not always reflected by accompanying newspaper correspondents:

> Our force makes up well of officers and men, all well-equipped for the winter campaign, giving a bizarre appearance of hats, buffalo caps, keples [sic.], pouches, chiripas, etc., not very military, but very comfortable. Good humor is the order of the day. In an occasional dugout you may hear a disconsolate violin screeching out the trials of "Mollie darling," accompanied by a half-tuned banjo; or campaigning songs, interspersed with stories of gaucho narratives or personal adventure at the front; comments on the expedition, while at the same time, overcoats, caps, etc., have no fixed owners, and disappear in a manner that would puzzle Hermann, the wizard.
>
> The weather favors us, though bitterly cold in the morning — warms up during the afternoon and the boys crawl out for stables and guard mount. At night camp presents a gala appearance. In front of each tent is an improvised fireplace, and the bright light of burning cedar reflected on the white tents reminds us of war days. As I write, the mail has been distributed, and at every fire are crouched two or three men eagerly devouring the contents of their letters — some bewailing their luck at not getting any mail.[103]

By early April the last sullen and bedraggled bands had been cowed into returning to the reservations, and it was time to pronounce the punishment to be exacted from the guilty. The leading chieftains and tribesmen of the wayward hostiles were to be singled out and sent to prison at Fort Marion, Florida.[104]

During the campaign four white captives had been recovered from the warring tribes. These unhappy young ladies, the German girls who had been taken from their parents' homestead on the Smoky Hill River the past summer, were to identify the offending Cheyennes. After several tiring sessions during which only thirteen braves could be pointed out, the quota of thirty-three was reached by the arbitrary selection of twenty others.[105] It seemed that all were to be considered responsible and that one Indian would do equally well as another. The Kiowas made somewhat of a farce of the whole procedure by selecting their "guilty" from among the least prominent members of the tribe and from captured Mexicans who had been taken into their numbers as warriors.[106]

The Miles Campaign removed the last vestiges of the classic plains culture. The will to fight had been exacted from even the most inflexible who had held out to the end for the preservation of some semblance of the old way of life. Perhaps they reasoned that it was better after all to accept the distasteful reservation life that was offered and chance dying slowly rather than to continue the struggle and sustain the inevitable heavy losses of war.

During the summer of 1875 the buffalo hunters, who had impatiently awaited the army's chastisement of the Indians, moved onto the Staked Plains and commenced the slaughter anew. By 1878 the shooting was over, and the southern plains had been swept clean of the huge animals. Only the scattered bones of the fallen bison along the prairies remained to testify of the past. Like the red man himself, they had been found wanting within the expanding crucible of American civilization, and the glib reply so often advised by the frontier when queried on the problem of assimilating the Indians was offered for the buffalo — extermination.

CHAPTER V

COWBOYS AND SOLDIERS: THE LAST YEARS OF FORT DODGE

The Mature Post

The construction completed at Fort Dodge between 1865 and 1869 had done much to alleviate the misery of the enlisted men and provide at least minimal facilities for the storage of garrison supplies; however, the quarters provided for the post's officers remained rather primitive. After an inspection tour of the frontier posts had been completed in 1870, General Pope bluntly criticized the practice of housing officers in dugouts and crude frame buildings and immediately petitioned his military superiors to provide the needed funds to construct suitable quarters:

> The conditions of some of the officers at Fort Dodge is deplorable, living in holes dug in the ground, and covered with poles and mud. The quarters herein specified are absolutely needed and I hope and believe there will be no delay in giving the necessary authority to put up these quarters. I have just returned from Fort Dodge and will, I hope, be excused for expressing myself with such warmth after seeing officers and their families living in holes not fit to be dog kennels.[1]

Between 1870 and 1875 ten "sets" of quarters were constructed with a capacity to accommodate twenty officers and their families. Four of these sets or duplex structures were erected for captains. Each unit was considered to be a story and a half, as the attics were reserved for sleeping rooms. The dimensions of the quarters were forty-four by forty feet, thereby providing each family with eight hundred eighty square feet of living space on the ground floor. A dining room, parlor, kitchen and one bedroom were included on the ground floor.

The buildings were laid up with adobe and then covered with pine siding. Past experience had indicated that stone structures, although exceedingly durable, were much too expensive and tedious to erect. Common cedar shingles for roofing completed the shell of the quarters. Each unit was provided with a latrine and water barrel and enclosed in a picket fence.

The remaining six sets of quarters were added for lieutenants, with the same one and one-half story planning; however, the dimensions of these buildings were only thirty-five by thirty-two feet, thus leaving slightly more than five hundred square feet for each family. The lieutenants' quarters also included four rooms on the ground level, although they were necessarily somewhat smaller than those provided for captains.[2]

During the same span of time two single story frame apartment buildings were completed for civilian employees and their families. The accommodations thus provided were less spacious than those reserved for officers. Each family was assigned only two rooms, a kitchen and a second room which served for all other purposes.[3]

Three frame structures of varying dimensions were raised to serve the needs of the post's craftsmen. In addition to laboring in the shops of these buildings, the men stored the supplies of their several skills, such as paint, lumber and hardware within the facilities and also found space for living quarters for themselves and many of the post's teamsters.[4]

The fort's corrals were enlarged on several occasions to a final rectangle of three hundred thirty-six feet by two hundred twenty-one feet. The area was subdivided into cavalry, quartermaster, and quartermaster field corrals. The corral complex included a saddle room, stables and store rooms for each of the separate divisions. A granary with a capacity of a million pounds, capable of providing subsistence for the post's animals for a full year, was erected near the corrals.[5]

A small frame "dead house" was built opposite the hospital to receive fatalities before they were interred at the post cemetery. One of the last facilities erected was a more suitable guardhouse, which was completed in 1875, shortly after the older structure had been condemned as a result of a quartermaster inspection. Three driven wells fitted with hand pumps were situated within the area holding the majority of the living quarters, and the water wagons were thereafter relegated to the corrals.[6]

During the 1870's, trail herds from Texas were driven north to Dodge City for sale and shipment east on the Atchison, Topeka and Santa Fe Railroad. The cattle were often grazed near the town for several days or perhaps weeks before a mutually satisfactory price could be reached by the trail boss and one of the numerous buyers who met them at the end of the tracks. During this period the herds were pastured near the post, and as a result it quickly became necessary to assign a permanent cavalry detail to the task of keeping the hungry animals off the reservation.

On several occasions wandering steers had invaded the garrison, trampling over fences, pulling laundry down and putting to flight soldiers who contested the grounds with the cantankerous "longhorns." One herd, driven by an intense rainstorm, occupied the front porches of the officer's residences and were quite reluctant to vacate the shelter until the storm abated.[8] Perhaps even more offensive than the animals themselves was the aromatic residue they left behind.

As a result a board fence was erected around the entire perimeter of the post to deny the cattle entry onto the main grounds. The enlisted men viewed the new fence with mixed emotions, questioning which was the lesser of two evils: tolerating the trail herds or periodically white-washing the long spans of pine boards.[9]

As the Department of War was uncertain as to the future utility of the post after 1875, no major construction was undertaken after that date. The

Quartermaster Department considered enlarging the post several times, but on each such instance the Department of the Missouri successfully petitioned the Secretary of War to defer further construction until the question of the necessity of permanently maintaining the fort had first been settled.[10]

Peacetime Soldiering

Between the firing of the last shots of the Miles Campaign of 1874 and 1875, and the closing of Fort Dodge as a military installation in 1882, the garrison settled down to duties of military routine. Except for the Dull Knife Raid of 1878, and occasional invasions into Kansas by small hunting or trading parties from the Indian Territory to the south, the garrison's frontier wars were over.

The primary field duties of the post were to carry out scouts and patrols along the Arkansas River. From 1878 until 1880 they were occasionally assisted at this task by Kansas militia units, who roamed the southern border awaiting the entry of raiding parties into the state.[11] In addition to guarding the frontier, details were regularly assigned to escort wagons on their runs to both the north and south of the railroad depot at Dodge City during the process of delivering supplies and mail.[12] One such detachment, enroute to Camp Supply, came upon what appeared at a distance to be the bodies of several men hanging from trees. The officer in charge, sensing danger and unwilling to risk ambush with only four other soldiers present, immediately secured reinforcements. However, closer investigation proved most embarrassing. The dangling "men" were found to be nothing more than the laundry of several startled cowboys who had placed their clothes in the trees to dry.[13]

For the most part the civilian population proved much more unruly than the Indians during the fort's late years. By 1878 some one hundred thousand head of cattle were being driven to Dodge City annually. Open warfare frequently broke out between area ranchers and trail hands who were moving livestock into Kansas. The trail herds often carried Texas fever, which readily contaminated local animals. The trail bosses were seldom known for their courtesy, and they often drove their cattle through the fences and crops of irate local citizens. As a result, ranchers in the area of the post banded together and demanded heavy "tolls" of the Texans for the privilege of crossing private property on the way to the rail head. Occasionally the disputes over the right of passage erupted into gun battles, and the army was forced to mediate.[14]

As local frontier law enforcement became more effective, the garrison was called upon less frequently to join in searches for fleeing criminals. Dodge City's illustrious stalwarts of the badge, such as Wyatt Earp, Charlie Bassett, and Bat Masterson, usually chose the posse over the military detachment when help was needed. The poor relations which often existed between local cowboys and soldiers undoubtedly persuaded sheriffs and marshals that it was not advisable to mix the two. A good portion of the friction between civilian and military officials emanated from the increased incidence of vigilante law in western Kansas. These self-appointed guardians of law and order had frequently dealt out harsh summary "justice" to the garrison's enlisted men as well as to suspected civilian violators.[15]

In spite of the raw social atmosphere which existed in the area of the post, several soldiers took up homesteads near Dodge City. Usually the men waited until they had been discharged from the service before filing on land; however, several soldiers successfully claimed quarter sections while still in uniform. They accomplished this feat by recording their claims at the United States Land Office at Larned, Kansas, a small community just east of Fort Larned, without admitting their present status as enlisted men.[16] During leave, or if the claim was close to the post, during leisure hours, the men "proved up" their land and awaited the time when final title would be granted.

Cowboys and Soldiers

The near proximity of Dodge City to Fort Dodge inevitably led to frequent visits by the soldiers to the "frontier Babylon" and just as inevitably to numerous altercations between soldiers and cowboys. Barkeeps, prostitutes, gamblers, buffalo hunters and lawmen, who had usually spent considerable time on both sides of the law, added to the boisterous nature of the cowtown; but it was most often the trail hand who engaged the soldier in fisticuffs or shooting matches.

The occupations of most of the residents of Dodge City left considerable time available for leisure, and the "sport" of affronting "blueboys" came to be a favorite pastime.[17] Unlike the situation that existed between most frontier posts and nearby towns, where the soldiers were often berated for disorderly conduct and abusive treatment of the local citizenry, the dwellers at Dodge City proved more than capable of holding their own with the most belligerent troopers. In fact, it was the soldiers who most frequently complained that they could not enter the town without being tormented or molested by rowdy cowboys. One group of military visitors complained that not only were they affronted by local toughs, but that the town's guardians of law and order usually took the part of the aggressors rather than their own.

> When we arrived here a few months since and made the rounds about town, we had the fortune of getting acquainted with some of the best class citizens, and with pleasure changed our mind in regard to the respectability of Dodge City in general, and thought it would become quite a resort to relieve us at times of the monotony of garrison life, but since we find to our regret that a visitor still runs the risk of encountering the rudeness of the border ruffian, without any hope for redress, except one's own muscular strength. Especially are visiting soldiers made the objects of insults and sneers by those rowdies who delight in the disgraceful sport of getting brave and more honorable men than themselves in conflict with the city laws.
>
> The garrison of the Fort greatly donating to the prosperity of the town, we consider it the duty of the city authorities to protect visitors against those who have long forgotten what decency and respectability is. This can

> only be accomplished by selecting for their guardians of the peace men of strict impartiality and a high sense of honor. Meanwhile we would advise our fellow soldiers when visiting places of amusement in town, to confine themselves to places where gentlemanly proprietors will allow no impositions to be practiced upon them by the slums of town. Signed, Visiting Soldiers.[18]

Occasionally disagreements between troopers and cattle drovers precipitated spirited exchanges of gunfire, yet only a few men lost their lives during such contests. One disgruntled group of soldiers who had been fleeced of their money and then forcibly thrown out of a "gaming house" reported the incident to their company commander, who decided that it was time for the locals to be reminded of the fighting potency of the garrison.

After waiting out the following night when the proprietors and patrons of the house were expecting reprisal, the officer marched his men in formation to the vicinity of the saloon during the late hours of the second night. With most of the patrons already retired the officer dispersed his men as a firing squad, ordering several volleys discharged broadside into the establishment. Although no casualties were inflicted, perhaps because the troopers were ordered to aim too high to strike the occupants, the local residents quickly developed a healthy respect for the retaliatory capacities of the army.[19]

In 1877, after receiving numerous reports on the mistreatment of his men, Colonel William H. Lewis gathered his troopers and marched on the city. The local newspaper editor noted that as the columns approached Dodge City, "a pale gray look came over the faces" of several local rowdies and that "their chins quivered." He thought it ironical that a citizenry that had fought Indians and frequent gun duels was so obviously cowed by a modest military detachment.

The day was saved when the town judge intervened under a white flag. After the differences of the belligerents had been arbitrated to the satisfaction of all concerned, the colonel was escorted to the Dodge House and liberally treated to the city's best liquid hospitality.[20]

During one of Colonel Richard I. Dodge's tours of duty as commander of the post, his personal servant, a young Negro man, was shot to death while loading goods on a wagon, and his body was left lying on the streets until it was later retrieved by a military detachment. The infuriated officer notified the governor of Kansas that the town was run by a "band of vigilantes that exercise a complete tyranny of terror over good citizens." He threatened to take the town by storm; however, he abandoned his plans for revenge when notified that the slayers had already left Dodge City. As a result of the killing, Colonel Dodge helped to organize a Vigilance Committee. This group evolved into the eventually famous, and notorious Dodge City Peace Commission and later included Wyatt Earp, Luke Short, Charlie Bassett, and Bat Masterson on its rolls.[21]

Frequently it was good natured "horseplay" that motivated the cowboy to persecute the soldier. Such was the case in 1876 when Sergeant Jerome Weinberg, a non-commissioned signal officer, felt compelled to defend his honor and that of the army by accepting the challenge to participate in a gun duel. The young trooper was unusually amiable and was therefore well liked by both his fellow soldiers and a majority of the residents of Front Street in Dodge City. He was considered to be somewhat of an intellectual as, unlike his comrades, the sergeant possessed a high school education.

While he was escorting one of the town's young ladies home after a dance one night, he was confronted by a drunken pleasure-seeking drover, who put him to panicky flight toward Fort Dodge by firing several shots into the ground near his feet. The sight of the sergeant scurrying down Front Street with bullets striking close behind so captivated those watching that a plot was hatched to carry the harassment one step further. Included in the conspirators were several of Sergeant Weinberg's fellow troopers from the fort. Their task was to convince the sergeant that his honor had been insulted and that he would certainly lose the favor of his young lady friend if he did not accept the challenge of his tormentor and face him in a gun fight.

Another member of the conspirators was the local telegraph operator, George W. Birney. The telegrapher forged a message from the Commander of the Department of the Missouri, General Pope, to Sergeant Weinberg advising him that the general had been notified of his disgraceful display of cowardice and that he should challenge the local rowdy to a duel, thereby upholding the honor of himself and more importantly that of the entire army. While the sergeant was painfully weighing the dilemma of dishonor and possible death, the plot leaked out to the commander of Fort Dodge. As a result of the prank, the telegrapher was fired for forging the message from General Pope, and the military personnel involved escaped general courts-martial only after convincing the commander that they had no intention of allowing the sergeant to face the cowhand in an actual duel.[22]

Fortunately for the men of the garrison, they were not always the butt of the local citizenry's pranks. They enjoyed the harassment of "green horns" as thoroughly as did the trail hands. Several troopers were on hand on one occasion when a Kansas City "drummer" or traveling salesman named Elias Cohn made the mistake of elaborating too vividly on his exploits in the past as an Indian fighter. As a result, several of the local citizens invited the self-proclaimed frontiersman to accompany them on a raid against a party of Indians supposedly camped within a few miles of the city.

Unknown to the drummer, a second party of men who were dressed in Indian clothing which one of the local merchants kept on hand to sell as souvenirs to those passing through Dodge City, preceded the party of "Indian fighters" to a pre-arranged destination on the prairie. As the group of riders including the salesman approached the chosen spot, the cry of "Indians, ride for your life!" was emitted, and all of the drummer's companions, who were considerably better horsemen than he, rode off in different directions, leaving the startled Indian fighter alone on the prairie.

No sooner had he lost sight of the last galloping horse than he was beset by an attacking band of howling "Indians." The drummer rode as quickly as possible in the direction of Dodge City, but the band of hostiles not only followed him to within sight of the city, they continued the pursuit to the very door of a local dry goods merchant where the salesman sought refuge. The local editor noted that the drummer left Dodge City without again mentioning his talents for handling Indians and that in the future another representative was sent by his company to service the Dodge City area.[23]

Two of the favorite saloons of both the drover and the soldier in Dodge City were the Saratoga and the Long Branch. Here gambling, drinking and prostitution were made available to the patrons. Although both gambling and prostitution were declared illegal during the late 1870's, the practice of both continued unabated. In fact, they were made illegal not to stamp them out, but to raise revenue for the use of the city.[24]

Dodge City soon found that law officers willing to brave the hazards of Front Street were expensive, and the reasoning of the "town gentry" was that the gaming houses should be required to share the expense of city government, especially since it was their establishments that necessitated the retention of several lawmen. Once gambling and prostitution had been declared illegal, the proprietors could be "fined" periodically, thereby providing a lucrative source of city finance.

Occasionally athletic contests were held in Dodge City or at Fort Dodge. In 1877, the Fort Dodge Clippers baseball team lost to the Dodge City Club 19 to 15 and shortly thereafter lodged a bitter protest that several members of the Dodge City team had been drunk during the game. No explanation was offered as to exactly how inebriation had favorably enhanced the athletic prowess of the cow town team.[25]

That same year a prize fight under bare knuckle rules was fought in the streets. According to one of the witnesses the contest was an epic affair:

> On last Tuesday morning the champion prize fight of Dodge City was indulged in by Messrs. Nelson Whitman and the noted Red Hanley, familiarly known as "the red bird from the South." An indefinite rumor had been circulated in sporting circles that a fight was to take place, but the time and place was known only to a select few. The sport took place in front of the Saratoga, at the silent hour of 4:30 a.m. when the city police were retiring after the dance hall revelry had subsided and the belles who reign were off duty. Promptly at the appointed time the two candidates for championship were at the joint. Colonel Norton acted as rounder up and whipper-in for both fighters, while Bobby Gill ably performed the arduous task of healing and handling and sponging off. Norton called "time" and the ball opened with some fine hits from the shoulder. Whitman was the favorite in the pools, but Red made a brilliant effort to win the champion belt. During the forty-second round Red Hanley implored Norton to take Nelson off for a little while till he could have time to put his right eye back where it belonged, set his jaw bone and have the ragged edge trimmed off his ears where they had been

chewed the worst. This was against the rules of the ring, so Nelson declined, encouraging him to bear it as well as he could and squeal when he got enough. About the sixty-first round Red squealed unmistakable, and Whitman was declared the winner. The only injuries sustained by the loser in this fight were two ears chewed off, one eye bursted and the other disabled, right cheek bone caved in, bridge of the nose broken, seven teeth knocked out, one jaw bone mashed, one side of the tongue chewed off, and several other unimportant fractures and bruises. Red retires from the ring in disgust.[26]

Entertainment, whiskey, cardsharps, prostitutes and occasionally violent death awaited the frontier soldier in Dodge City. Before his death, Bob Wright frequently told the story of a drunken cowboy who stumbled onto a train in Kansas City and immediately lapsed into a deep sleep. When he was rudely awakened by the conductor and queried as to his anticipated destination, he sullenly replied "to Hell," and went back to sleep. Early the next morning the drover was again rousted out of his sleep and told he had arrived, and he stepped off the train into the streets of Dodge City.[27]

The Dull Knife Flight of 1878

"We Are Hungry"

During the summer of 1877 a large band of approximately one thousand Northern Cheyennes moved southward via Fort Dodge on their way to the Indian Territory. The Cheyennes were being transferred from the Red Cloud Agency of the Dakotas under government supervision. They had participated in the Battle of the Little Big Horn the preceding year, and several of the braves still wore clothing taken while counting coup against the men of General Custer's U. S. Seventh Cavalry.

While the Indians camped near Fort Dodge in late July before moving on to Camp Supply, many of the residents of Dodge City turned out to take advantage of what they supposed to be one of their last opportunities to view the red man in his natural state. Before their journey was continued, many of the Cheyenne returned the visit by spending several days in the town begging on a door-to-door basis and periodically performing native dances for the gratification of their curious hosts.[28]

Unknown to the Dodge Citians, they would later have a second opportunity to see many of these same Indians, but under considerably less amiable circumstances. The Cheyennes had been reluctant to abandon their home in the north and had finally agreed to do so only after obtaining the assurance of several of their leading chiefs, including Standing Elk, Dull Knife, Wild Hog and Little Wolf, that they had received the government promise that the tribe would be well provided with annuities in the south and that they could return to their northern hunting grounds if their home within the Indian Territory near Fort Reno proved unsatisfactory.[29]

One year near Fort Reno proved to be quite enough for the Cheyennes.

The terrain and climate of the new reservation were quite different from that to which the Indian had been accustomed, and many sickened and died shortly after their arrival. Most grievous of all of the band's complaints was the tardy and inadequate delivery of promised annuities. The Cheyennes spent much of the winter of 1877 living hand to mouth, and the suffering experienced during these bleak months convinced the Indians that they must return to their northern home or slowly perish within the confines of the barren wastes of the south.[30]

Their agent at Fort Reno persuaded them to remain during the summer; but as fall approached and they were forced to anticipate a second winter with no game to hunt and their annuity supplies undependable, a decision was reached. In early September Dull Knife and Little Wolf informed the reservation authorities that some three hundred of their people, including approximately seventy braves, had decided to return north.[31] They were immediately told that such action would not be tolerated and that their flight would be intercepted by troops before they had gained the Kansas border. This threat proved to be ineffective. The Cheyennes replied that they would sooner die quickly at the hands of the army than to submit to the perils of continued reservation life in the south, and struck out northward along the north fork of the Canadian River.[32]

All of the military posts to the north along the anticipated line of march of the Indians were immediately advised of the Cheyennes' departure and ordered to prepare to send troops into the field to halt the wayward band. The Cheyennes had persuaded the military that they would fight rather than return peaceably, and the small detachment of troops garrisoned at Fort Reno chose to shadow the Indians rather than to engage them before adequate reinforcements could be sent from Camp Supply and Fort Dodge.[33]

As the ranking field officer in western Kansas and the Western Indian Territory, Colonel William Lewis, the Commander of Fort Dodge, was ordered to assume responsibility for stopping the Cheyennes. He was first advised of the approximate location and direction of travel of the band on September 11, when scouts reported them to be moving toward the Kansas border, approximately twenty miles north of Camp Supply.[34] The colonel responded by dispatching two cavalry companies under the separate commands of Captains Rendlebrook and Hemphill to Sand Creek and Bear Creek, both directly south of Fort Dodge and just north of the Kansas border, to engage the Indians.[35]

On September 13, Captain Rendlebrook's company was surprised and mauled near Sand Creek when they were attacked while moving through a ravine. The Cheyennes completely surrounded the cavalrymen and kept them pinned down for a day and a half while their women and children continued the march northward. Three men of the company were killed and three others wounded during the brisk engagement. Late on September 14 the company escaped and immediately retreated to Fort Dodge.[36]

Two days later Captain Hemphill's company found and engaged the Cheyennes, who were by then only forty miles south of Fort Dodge. After several half-hearted charges during which only one man was wounded, the cavalrymen disengaged and commenced following the Indians, hopeful that reinforcements would be send to bolster the command.[37]

Prior to the skirmishes with Captain Hemphill's company, the Indians had refrained from raiding any of the numerous ranches they had passed while moving through southern Kansas. Only a few cows had been killed for food during the march. Unfortunately for the settlers of western Kansas, several cattlemen were noticed riding with Captain Hemphill's command, thereby convincing the Cheyennes that the ranchers had taken up arms against them.[38]

After the clash with Captain Hemphill, the Cheyennes split up into several small bands and initiated a series of atrocities as they continued their flight. Several large trail herds on their way to Dodge City, which were found along the path of the Indian, were raided and a number of drovers were killed and mutilated. Many of the trail hands abandoned their livestock and rode for Dodge City while others sought out the military detachments operating in the area and joined forces with them.[39]

Although Captain Hemphill's detachment was eventually complemented by the addition of seventy or eighty well armed drovers, he refused to attack even the smallest of the bands of Cheyenne operating south of Fort Dodge. On one occasion his troops drew too close to a party of some thirty warriors which they had been following, and when the Cheyennes abruptly turned and charged the startled troopers and cowboys, they panicked and gave up the field ingloriously without having fired a shot.[40]

The combination of demands for effective action from the Department of the Missouri and the repeated ineptness and cowardice displayed by his officers in the field so irritated Colonel Lewis that he recalled the detachments on September 20 and assumed personal command.[41] Captains Rendlebrook and Hemphill were both later convicted of cowardice and dismissed from the army.[42]

By September 20, numerous reports of the sighting of roaming bands of Cheyennes had reached Dodge City and the citizens feverishly prepared to receive the expected assault. Their efforts were quickened by the news that several citizens had been massacred to the southwest, near Meade City, and that the town had been saved only after offering several dressed beeves to the hungry Indians.[43] A locomotive was kept constantly ready at the depot, and periodically a number of well armed men boarded the train to scout along the tracks to both the east and the west of the town.[44] When a fire broke out on a farm near the southern edge of the city limits on September 21, the residents were sure that the anticipated battle had commenced; however, further investigation by Wyatt Earp and several of his comrades indicated that the blaze had been started by an unattended stove rather than by the Cheyennes.[45]

The mayor of Dodge City, James Kelley, discovered that only twenty-seven men remained at Fort Dodge while their fellow troopers were in the field searching for the Indians, and fearing that Dodge City would not be protected, he wired the governor for rifles to arm the local citizens.[46] The governor hesitated at first, perhaps finding it difficult to believe that a town which had existed by the gun needed more of the same, but eventually the requested weapons were forwarded and distributed among the men. Ironically several months later, after the Cheyenne scare had subsided and their was no further danger of attack, the governor was forced to threaten legal action before he could persuade the mayor to collect and return the weapons to the state arsenal.[47]

While Dodge City braced itself for an attack which never came, Colonel Lewis gathered every available man, to a total of five companies of cavalry, and boarded a train for the Cimarron where a large band of the Cheyennes had reportedly crossed between the 21st and 23rd of September.[48] He arrived there on the 25th and, after unloading his men, horses and supplies, commenced a forced march northward along the trail left by the Cheyennes. The intelligence reports gathered by his scouts indicated that most of the roaming bands had rendezvoused at the Cimarron before continuing to move northward.

The colonel, anxious to redeem the good name of the command after the mediocre performance of his troops south of Fort Dodge, pressed the pursuit steadily until the Cheyennes were located on September 27, on the Punished Woman's Fork of the Smoky Hill River, some thirty miles south of Fort Wallace. The Indians, exhausted by the long weeks of sustained flight, and suffering greatly from hunger and exposure, dug in along the walls of a ravine and prepared to give battle.[49]

Colonel Lewis deployed his men for a final assault, which he hoped would bring an end to the embarrassing odyssey of his elusive prey. The colonel, apparently somewhat skeptical of the fighting mettle of the command, moved from company to company exhorting the cavalrymen to uphold the honor of the service as the scheduled time of the assault approached. His scouts repeatedly warned him that exposing his person to the gunsights of the waiting Cheyennes was foolhardy, but the gritty officer persisted, undoubtedly hoping that his own examples of open disdain for the fighting prowess of the Indians might spur his men into giving a good account of themselves once the shooting started.[50]

During the initial attempt to storm the Cheyennes by force and dislodge them from the protection of the natural stronghold, the colonel and three enlisted men were quickly shot down. The sight of Colonel Lewis falling before the Cheyennes suddenly depleted what little appetite his men had held for combat, and the command quickly retired to the safety of the rear camp.[51] During this brief skirmish the scouts had succeeded in capturing sixty ponies from the Indians' lightly guarded herd, but the Cheyennes themselves emerged from the contest relatively unscathed.[52]

While the command's junior officers debated the proper tactics for a second attempt at overrunning the ravine, which was to be made on the following day, their quarry slipped out of their entrenchments under the cover of darkness and continued the journey northward. News was received the next morning that their colonel had died while being moved to Fort Wallace for medical attention. The bullet had struck the veteran soldier in the thigh, rupturing the femoral artery, and he had bled to death before a surgeon's help could be obtained.[53]

The report that the Cheyennes had once more escaped was quickly carried to Fort Wallace and Fort Hays, and troops were deployed along the Kansas Pacific Railroad from both posts to intercept the band.[54] Shortly after their departure from Punished Woman's Fork, the Indians split into two groups, one led by Dull Knife and the other under Little Wolf.[55] In addition to this major separation of forces, several small scouting parties were sent out to reconnoiter the path of flight.

The diffusion of the Indians intensely complicated the task of the searching troopers. The confusing flood of reports that reached the cavalrymen as to the location of the Cheyennes indicated that they were spread along a route of travel roughly fifty to seventy-five miles wide. Before either of the major bands could be found, they had crossed the Kansas Pacific and quickly escaped into Nebraska.[56]

The exodus of the Indians across the prairie and the frustrating attempts of the army to corral them drew increasing attention from newspaper editors and humanitarians across the country.[57] The temptation to support the courage of the "underdog" undoubtedly enlivened the debate, and considerable evidence was made public that the Indians had been driven to attempt escape from Indian Territory by the deplorable conditions they had experienced near Fort Reno. Amos Chapman, a respected frontiersman who spoke with considerable authority on matters relevant to the Indian, stated that upon visiting the reservation shortly before the flight of the Cheyennes, he had found them existing on the carcasses of putrified horses.[58] Others argued that the gallant struggle of the Indians deserved something better than being forced to return to the Indian Territory and that the army should give up the search and allow the Cheyennes to remain in the north.[59]

The residents of southwestern Kansas were less sentimental in their proposal. Several settlers and cattle drovers had died at the hands of the migrant red men, and they were unwilling to settle for anything less than an eye for an eye. The Cheyennes had committed murder within the borders of Kansas, it was argued, and they should be returned to the state to stand trial for their atrocities as would other criminals.[60]

While the debate over the thorny problem continued, Little Wolf's band settled down on Lost Chokecherry Creek in central Nebraska where, undiscovered by the army, they subsisted on small game and waited the coming of warm weather.[61] Dull Knife's people were less fortunate. After having traveled several hundred miles, they were discovered in extreme northwestern Nebraska by two companies of cavalry from Fort Robinson. Ironically the Indians were within fifty miles of the safety of both the Wyoming Territory and the Sioux Reservation of the Dakota Territory.[62]

Dull Knife's warriors were convinced that once having reached this far north, the government would relent and agree to allow them to remain on their old hunting grounds. The band was quartered in empty barracks at the fort while the War Department wrestled with the dilemma of what to do with them. If they were sent back to Indian Territory, the army could anticipate a scathing barrage of public condemnation. However, if the Cheyennes were permitted to rejoin their northern kinsmen, a dangerous precedent might be set, and every discontented band in the south could be expected to take note of the Cheyennes' successful flight and attempt to escape to the north the following summer.[63]

After two months of debate the army reached a decision. On January 3, 1879, orders were received at Fort Robinson to escort the unhappy plainsmen back to Indian Territory.[64] The Cheyennes accepted the news of their fate stoically; however, they refused to leave their barracks to assemble for removal back to the Fort Reno Agency. Food, blankets and firewood were withheld from the determined band; and even though the temperature sank to several degrees below zero, they stubbornly remained huddled in the barracks.[65]

On January 10, two of their chiefs, Wild Hog and Old Crow, were placed in solitary confinement, convincing their remaining kinsmen that they were shortly to be forcibly taken southward. That night, armed with several rifles they had concealed after their arrival at Fort Robinson, a party of braves attacked the guards and held off pursuit until the main body of the Cheyennes had escaped toward the frigid bluffs north of the post.[66] The Indians paid a bitter price for their short-lived freedom. Of approximately one hundred and seventy men, women and children who had fled, thirty-five were killed during the first hours after the revolt and a like number were brought back to the fort wounded.[67]

It was not until January 21, that the last party was captured, and at that Dull Knife and his family had escaped to Pine Ridge Agency to the north. A final tally indicated that only fifty-eight of the Cheyennes had survived the struggle with the army. Most of these were women and children, and many were sick or wounded by the hardships of the stay at Fort Robinson. Only seven warriors were considered fit to stand trial for the transgressions of the band.[68]

The State of Kansas vs. Wild Hog, et al.

During the month of December while Dull Knife's band was being held in barracks at Fort Robinson, Michael W. Sutton, Ford County Attorney of Dodge City, labored diligently to persuade Governor Anthony to seek extradition of the Cheyennes so that they might be tried as criminals within Kansas.[69] Sutton argued that a precedent for prosecution had been established by Texas in 1871, where the Kiowa Chiefs Satanta and Big Tree had been convicted of murder and sentenced to be hanged.[70]

The Kiowas had escaped the hangman's noose when President Grant, responding to Eastern pressure for clemency, had successfully petitioned Texas Governor Edmund J. Davis to commute the sentences to life imprisonment. In October, 1873, Governor Davis incurred the wrath of his constituency, and more important, that of the Texas State Legislature, by granting Satanta and Big Tree full pardons and ordering them released from the Texas State Prison.[71]

Attorney Sutton, a stalwart Republican, immediately sensed the political potential that could be his if he should successfully prosecute the Cheyennes in a state that had long considered extermination the obvious solution to the Indian problem. Sutton realized the difficulty of finding witnesses who could identify the guilty and decided to charge Dull Knife's entire band with murder in the first degree.[72] Unfortunately all those who could have perhaps provided positive identification of the actual killers had died at the hands of the guilty.

Governor Anthony relayed Sutton's petition for extradition to J. H. Hammond, who held the post of United States Indian Inspector within the Department of the Interior, and on December 6, 1878, the inspector consented to allow Kansas authorities to try the Cheyennes under the stipulation that only those actually involved in killing be prosecuted and not the entire band.[73] The state of Nebraska quickly consented to allow the Cheyennes to be extradited without protest, and on February 11, Sheriff Bat Masterson, several deputies and a group of witnesses presented themselves at Fort Leavenworth to identify the guilty from among seven Cheyenne warriors sent there from Nebraska.[74]

All seven were immediately accused by the witnesses of having been present at one or several of the six murders recorded the past fall, and they were released along with their families, which totaled fourteen women and children, into the custody of Sheriff Masterson for removal to Ford County where they would await trial.[75] As the sheriff and his charges made their way westward along the Atchison, Topeka and Santa Fe Railroad, curious crowds turned out at nearly every depot stop in hopes of seeing the "murdering savages."[76] After their arrival at Dodge City, a steady stream of local citizens visited the county jail to look the Cheyennes over. Occasionally the prisoners were taken outside to pose in front of the court house with town gallants who wanted to be photographed with Indians.[77]

The gross mistreatment of the Cheyennes in 1878, from the trek of the hungry band through Kansas to the circus trial which was shaping up in Dodge City, was unpalatable even to a staunch Indian hater such as Nicholas Klaine, the fiery and locally influential editor of the *Dodge City Times:* "We are about to begin to change our sentiment in regard to the Indians. We believe the process of starving him a cruel and barbarous practice." Klaine asked for a less gaudy but equally effective approach in dealing with wayward Indians: "Killing the Indians by starvation is against our ideas of Indian extinction. We believe the speedy method of slaughter the most expeditious. The best Indian is a dead Indian."[78]

Klaine's dubious brand of "sympathy" for the redman changed abruptly, however, under the increasingly heated condemnation of the impending trial which was building in the East:

> The transfer of the seven Cheyenne bucks from the military to the civil authorities has aroused an intense feeling throughout the country. Now that the gentle savage is to be tried for the crimes committed on this border, we shall look for a superabundance of gushing sentimentality; a mawkish feeling that overtakes those who know but little of Indian trait or character.

> The question of identity will add to the sympathetic fervor that finds a lodgement in many minds, but that identity is already confirmed in those who know a Cheyenne buck from a prairie wolf. The particular Indians may have smote the earth at Fort Robinson. The seven now in jail, however, are accessory to the enormous crimes committed on this border last September. The proof lies in the bones now bleaching on the plains.[79]

County Attorney Sutton prepared his case laboriously. Every available hostile witness was summoned for the June trial, and General Pope, who still commanded the Department of the Missouri, was asked to serve as interpreter for the Cheyennes.[80] The Indians were represented by able Eastern attorneys retained by sympathetic humanitarians who suspected the Cheyennes would be convicted after a mockery of justice.[81]

During the opening stages of the trail, before Sutton had the opportunity to present his case, his Eastern colleague's legal dexterity was applied with unexpectedly damaging results. The counsel for the Cheyennes argued that a fair trial could not be given the prisoners in such a hostile setting as that existing in Dodge City, and the trial judge ruled that a change of venue should be granted.[82]

Sutton's case burst before his eyes like an overextended bubble. Few of his witnesses could be persuaded to attend the new trial scheduled at Lawrence in Douglas County. Those who did appear found the inquiries of the defense attorneys immediately embarrassing. It became obvious during the early moments of the new trial that the witnesses could not tell one Indian from another, and without positive identification the proceedings could not be continued. The case was dismissed for lack of evidence against the accused.[83] On this note the bizarre trial of the Cheyennes ended, and they were sent south to their reservation to rejoin their families. A disgruntled Sutton returned with his witnesses and shattered case to Dodge City, convinced that a miscarriage of justice had deprived him of his quarry.

The Sentinel Retired

As early as 1878, General Pope petitioned the War Department to close Fort Dodge,[84] but the embarrassing intrusion of the Cheyennes into western Kansas shortly after his request was made persuaded his superiors that the post should be kept active until the final threat of invasions from the Indian Territory had been removed. The general considered that the frontier could be most satisfactorily served by eliminating all the forts along the Santa Fe and Smoky Hill Routes in Kansas. The garrisons of these forts were to be moved to other posts, such as Fort Sill and Fort Reno within the Indian Territory, and Fort Elliott in Texas, which were much closer to the several reservations that had been set apart for the southern tribes.[85]

General Pope's position found almost immediate favor with a great number of the most prominent political figures of Kansas who were receiving considerable constituency pressure to open several military reservations to settlement. In 1879, Senator Ingalls of Kansas introduced a bill before Congress which was designed to open approximately the northern two-thirds of the Fort Dodge reservation to homesteaders.[86] His colleagues quickly passed the bill; but before the lands could be claimed, the Department of the Interior challenged the enactment. Both the Senate and House of Representatives had acted favorably on the proposal because they considered the lands to be available for transfer to the Department of the Interior; however, Henry Price, a commissioner with the department found that part of the reservation had been carved from former Osage Reserve lands and that any funds accruing from their sale should be transferred to a trust fund for the tribe.[87]

This hurdle was overcome by simply ignoring the Osage claims, and on December 15, 1880, the lands were opened to settlement.[88] Of the first seventy-five claims filed on the lands, eighteen were by gamblers, saloon-keepers, bartenders and prostitutes from Dodge City, four by town widows, six by railroad employees, and only ten by actual settlers.[89] The remaining fourteen thousand acres of land, which included the post, were not opened until late in 1889, when a miniature reenactment of the Oklahoma rush took place as land hungry citizens sought to share in some of the last lands being opened to homesteaders.[90]

On April 5, 1882, the garrison at Fort Dodge was ordered to commence preparations for abandoning the post. All usable supplies and equipment that could be moved were to be freighted to Camp Supply.[91] Of the three companies of men stationed there, one was ordered to Fort Elliott, a second to Fort Reno and the third to Camp Supply. By the first of October the removal of the supplies and equipment had been completed, and the post records were crated and shipped to Fort Leavenworth. On October second, 1882, the flag was lowered and the last detachment of troops marched southward to Camp Supply.[92] The sentinel to the Cimarron had been retired.

CHAPTER VI

CONCLUSION: THE SENTINEL IN RETROSPECT

The Significance of the Location and Function of Fort Dodge

The rationale for establishing Fort Dodge on the Arkansas River along the Santa Fe Trail was dictated more by circumstances than by deliberate planning by the War Department. It was the commercial routes of the Southwest, the advancing settler's frontier and the presence of several Plains Indian tribes whose combined convergence at the Cimarron Crossing dictated that a post be erected in this locality. These factors tended to draw the military to the site as a pragmatic response to frontier needs rather than the fort's being erected as part of a greater plan to make the West safe for habitation. The military frontier arrived in western Kansas less as a vanguard to increase the perimeter of settlement, than as the tardy guardian of a commercial frontier already well established.

Without the huge territorial acquisitions which accrued to the United States as a result of the Mexican War, it is doubtful that Fort Dodge would have been erected. Although the soil of the area was fertile and easily accessible, marginal rainfall and the lack of farming skills capable of exploiting the area by the plow would undoubtedly have proven hurdles that the farming frontier would not have successfully passed until late in the 19th century or perhaps during the early years of the 20th.

Once the fort was established and some measure of protection to settlers could be provided, the farming frontier quickly invaded the prairies of western Kansas. The land acquisitions realized through the Treaty of Guadalupe Hidalgo created a demographically divided nation. Arteries of commerce, settlement and communication immediately became vital and the Santa Fe Trail had already proven itself as a viable route of service to the Southwest. Fort Dodge emerged during the post-Civil War era as the protector of a huge segment of the trail from Central Kansas westward into the Colorado Territory.

Of equal importance in assessing the significance of the military experience of the post were the limits of the Indian Territory. Prior to the establishment of Fort Dodge the frontier had moved steadily onto the plains in a westerly direction, but once the 100th meridian had been reached and the Plains tribes had been directed to remain south of the Arkansas River by the terms of the Treaty of Medicine Lodge Creek in 1867, the Kansas military frontier then pivoted, facing southward rather than westward. Fort Dodge became the anchor of the western flank of the central frontier and as such, the primary point of pressure to confine the Indians south of the Arkansas River.

Because the presence of the fort impeded the opportunity of the Indians to prey on the southern buffalo herd and to strike back at the white men along the vulnerable Santa Fe Trail, they consistently attempted to turn the western flank. Their success in so doing was invariably short lived and the redmen were methodically pressed backward along the line of the Arkansas River.

The success of Fort Dodge in holding the western flank was not without qualification. The commercial routes and the settler's frontier were both exposed to assault by the Plains Tribes on numerous occasions, yet the primary mission of the post was accomplished by 1882, as the last threat of invasion had been eliminated.

By holding the western sector of the frontier at the Arkansas River, Fort Dodge, along with her sister posts guarding the Santa Fe, Smoky Hill and Platte River Routes, opened a wide belt of communication, commerce and travel across the central plains and in so doing greatly reduced the isolation of West from East.

The neglect of the history of the military experience of Fort Dodge has resulted in relatively little consideration being given to the post's efforts during the campaigns carried out by General Hancock in 1867, by General Sheridan in 1868 and 1869, and by General Miles in 1874 and 1875. Although little was accomplished by the abortive march of General Hancock, the post, along with Fort Larned, served as a gathering point for negotiations with the several tribes then pursuing hostilities. In the wake of the campaigners' withdrawal from the plains, the environs of Fort Dodge bore the brunt of the general assault unleashed by the tribes in retaliation for Hancock's burning of the Cheyenne village.

During the campaigns of 1868-1869 and 1874-1875, the fort not only served as the focal point for commencing field operations but sustained the troops once they had moved to the south by supplying them during the long months of military operations. In both of these contests the strategy of chastizing the Indians was planned after consideration of intelligence reports gathered by the Fort Dodge garrison. Troops who became casualties of the campaigns were evacuated to the post's hospital. After each of the punitive marches had been completed the fort was handed the problem of maintaining security along the frontier according to the provisions of the agreements reached with the temporarily cowed but always resurgent Indians.

The modest accomplishments of each of the major campaigns waged on the southern plains served to place the major burden of containing the threat of retaliatory atrocities at the hands of the natives on the small garrisons of troops at the posts along the frontier. Fort Dodge accepted a heavy portion of that task. In the final analysis it was more the constant vigilance and tenacious field engagements of these posts than the colorful but rather ineffective major campaigns that reduced the threat of Indian invasion and depredation. The nature of the Indian in combat perhaps dictated that if he was to be beaten it would be by military detachments small enough to invite a contest. Women, children, ponies and homes could be obliterated easily by major campaigns, but the battle wise inhabitants of the plains would only accept combat engagement by units they could reasonably expect to defeat.

The task faced by Fort Dodge in helping to subdue the Plains tribes was greatly complicated by the ambiguity of the nation's Indian policy. During the same season of turmoil the post might serve as an instrument of chastizement and as the hand of appeasement. The same natives who looked to the post for annuities might be met by representatives of the fort within days or weeks on the field of combat.

What was perhaps the only viable solution — that of leaving the Indian in relative isolation to choose his own path of civilization — was judged unacceptable. The unquenchable thirst of the settlers for land forced the government to reduce constantly the lands of the Indian and in so doing, military engagement became inescapable. Once hostilities had been initiated, the task of the soldier became increasingly frustrating. He was expected to reduce militarily his adversary, yet no hero's welcome awaited him once his mission had been accomplished.

On the one hand, the Western press and the residents of the frontier welcomed the extermination of the redmen, while the Eastern press, humanitarians and a rapidly growing portion of public, speaking through Congress, asked for a more humane solution. Neither success nor failure in the field would satisfy the many publics reviewing the action of the army and on few occasions could the soldier be secure in the knowledge he had accomplished his mission according to the dictates of national policy. Such was the ambiguity of a policy of pragmatism.

In addition to the pitfalls of a vague and inconsistent plan for pacifying the Indians, the task of the soldier was further complicated within the local area of military responsibility by the greed and avarice of his fellow whites. No tabulation may be made with certainty in regard to the number of lives lost, red and white, as a result of the indiscriminate sale of arms and alcohol to the Indians by renegades, but without a doubt the loss was considerable. How much the nation must bear collective responsibility for the crude exploitation of the Indians is debatable, yet it becomes more difficult to judge the individual who cheated and exploited the redman when his acts were not inconsistent with those of the government. The agent who fraudulently withheld annuities, the trader who took advantage of the native's innocence and the buffalo hunter who slaughtered his staff of life, were undoubtedly comforted by the apparent lack of collective conscience evident within the nation's Indian policy.

The Legacy of Fort Dodge to American Military Heritage

The military history of Fort Dodge was partially shared with her sister posts along the frontier and partially unique because of the individual location and mission of the post. Like the other sentinel forts along the Santa Fe and Smoky Hill routes, the garrison experienced the monotony of isolation, the hazards of weather and Indian engagements and the back-breaking task of building and maintaining a military installation in a most exacting region. The field duties of Fort Dodge, with the exception of guarding the Cimarron and the line of the Arkansas River, were much the same as those of other Western forts.

In addition to traditional military responsibilities, Fort Dodge acted as the primary source of law and provisions for those journeying along the Santa Fe Trail. Wagons whose animals had been disabled or stolen found replacements at the post. Food and lodging were also extended to the needy; most often to white settlers, but on many occasions to destitute Indians.

Within the confines of the garrison, the soldiers played many roles. He could expect to be assigned to such tasks as sawing timber, cleaning stables, cooking company mess, constructing buildings, gathering garbage and a score of other chores during his enlistment. In return for his labor the government provided him with a modest wage, adequate living quarters, a marginal diet, medical attention, elementary education, a few recreational diversions and some guidance in his spiritual life.

Those who deviated from the code of conduct prescribed by military law could expect immediate disciplinary recourse to be taken by the garrison's officers. The penalties for the most serious offenses were usually handed down "by the book," but a degree of local interpretation is also evident in the administration of justice. The soldier found drunk or fighting usually escaped harsh treatment. The isolation and drudgery of soldiering on the plains drove an alarming number of enlisted men to desert and a certain amount of misconduct could perhaps be tolerated in light of the exacting circumstances experienced by the trooper while soldiering on the prairies.

It was perhaps to be expected that a considerable degree of innovation would be demonstrated by a garrison established in such a locale. The food placed on the tables at mess usually reflected the talent of the troops to forage, hunt and purchase supplementary foodstuffs from the surrounding area. The equipment provided by the army was often altered or discarded and replaced by items fashioned by the soldiers themselves to serve their immediate needs. The growth of the post itself, especially in regard to the facilities erected, reflected the needs of soldiers stationed in a situation of relative isolation.

Examination of the expanding military frontier in the west reveals that each post played a separate and unique role in the total mosaic of subduing the land and the natives, while acting as vanguard for the approaching settlers. As instruments of the expansion and final crystalization of American civilization in the West, the military forts and their personnel share in the plaudits that may be extended for having endured considerable hardship while extending the frontiers.

By 1882, Fort Dodge had ceased to be of value to the government as a military installation and the post was closed. In 1890, the United States Director of Census offered the opinion that the frontier no longer existed as an unbroken line across the territory of the nation. The military frontier, which had existed continually throughout the course of the United States' existence, soon ceased to be discernible and a colorful and essential chapter of American heritage had been completed.

EPILOGUE

THE SENTINEL RECHARTERED

Fort Dodge as a Soldier's Home

Following the closing of Fort Dodge as a military establishment in 1882, the post was placed under the authority of a caretaker appointed by the War Department. This position, which paid the holder seventy-five dollars per month, was eagerly sought by several aspirants. Secretary of War Lincoln, considered the position to fall under those to be filled through political patronage and appointed James Langton as the first custodian on the recommendation of the governor of Kansas.[1]

Mr. Langton tired of the monotony of watching over the fort and resigned his position in 1883, after having served for only one year.

Ironically, Robert M. Wright, a man whose exploitive talents in merchandising along the frontier had helped to precipitate clashes between the troops of the former garrison and the redmen, was appointed to be the next custodian. Wright's earlier business ventures, which included distribution of whiskey and speculation in buffalo hides, had returned handsome dividends, part of which had been invested in land close to the Fort Dodge reservation.[3] The opportunity to supplement his ranching income with the custodian's salary proved to be a minor windfall.

Wright opened the reservation lands, post buildings and corrals to cattle drovers and their herds while they awaited the sale of their cattle to Dodge City buyers.[4] The opening of these facilities was an obvious departure from traditional military policy, which denied public use of government reservations until they had been disposed of through proper channels.

During the summer months of 1886, several of the fort's officer dwellings were opened as temporary residences for smallpox victims. It was hoped that isolating the sick from those who remained healthy would curb the spread of the disease in nearby Dodge City.[5]

The first step toward final disposal of the fort was taken in 1884, when the War Department recommended that all reservation lands and facilities be transferred to the Department of the Interior; however, five years passed before Congress finally consented to the transfer of the land containing the buildings.[6] This same portion of the reservation was withheld from claim during a land rush late in 1889, during which the remainder of the lands were staked by settlers.[7]

The Kansas legislature had debated on several occasions whether or not to petition Congress for possession of the fort, to be utilized as a school for Indian children, but no positive action was taken. In 1888, the Methodist

College Association of southwestern Kansas asked permission of Congress to purchase the post grounds at a price of one dollar and twenty-five cents per acre. The Methodist College Association proposed to convert the fort into a liberal arts college.[8]

When the news of this petition reached Topeka, the Kansas legislature responded immediately by requesting Congress to donate the reservation to the state to be utilized as a state soldier's home. Congress acted favorably on the appeal of the Kansas legislature, but stipulated that the land was to be transferred at a cost of one dollar twenty-five cents per acre, rather than by donation as had been requested.[9] The citizens of Dodge City welcomed the opportunity to preserve the fort and soon collected the necessary funds for the purchase.[10] Six of the permanent quarters that had been built for officers, three barracks buildings, the hospital, the quartermaster building, the commissary storehouse and a number of smaller frame structures remained on the reservation to be used by the newly organized Kansas State Soldier's Home. Several of the frame buildings had already been razed by the army and the material taken to Camp Supply.[11]

By January 1, 1890, the soldier's home had been readied for occupancy.[12] The old troopers who were selected from numerous applicants to make their home at Fort Dodge undoubtedly experienced nostalgic reflection of their earlier days of service in the nation's armed forces on their arrival at the home. It was almost as if they had enlisted in the army again during their twilight years. A commander was appointed to supervise the home. Organization was on a military basis. Only men who had been residents of Kansas for at least two years, who were certified incapable of supporting or caring for themselves, and who had fought in one of the nation's past wars were admitted.[13]

Those with families or dependents were quartered in the old officer's homes or frame buildings. Children could be brought to Fort Dodge, however; boys, upon reaching fourteen years of age, and girls, upon reaching sixteen years of age, were required to leave their residence at the home.[14] Old soldiers who had remained single or were widowers were housed in the barracks.

Rations were allotted to each resident on a military basis. Those who violated the home's code of conduct, which was quite similar to the army's code of conduct, were brought before a review board and dismissed from residency when found guilty.[15] Deserters were considered absent without leave and dropped from the rolls.

Over ninety per cent of the first men admitted were Civil War veterans.[16] The remainder had served during the Mexican War or the Indian Wars. Some had military experience in more than one war. Former cavalryman Wesley Gall listed among the engagements in which he had participated, a charge against the Kiowas at the Cimarron and a campaign against the Sioux at Parode River, Wyoming in addition to several engagements of the Civil War.[17]

The first men admitted arrived at Fort Dodge in February, 1890. Although their military records indicated that they had served as members of military detachments from almost every state that had provided troops for the Union, the majority listed Iowa, Ohio, Pennsylvania, Illinois, Missouri or Indiana as the place of enlistment.[18] Many had taken up homesteads in Kansas following the war and in the years that followed had fulfilled the requirements of Kansas residency for admission.

Although most of the men were rather elderly, with sixty being an approximate average age, many proved to be immediate disciplinary problems. A number carried side arms as permitted by Kansas law. Whiskey was readily available at nearby Dodge City.

Of the first twenty men admitted, eight were dismissed the first year as violators of the home's code of conduct.[19] Twenty-five of the first one hundred were eventually dismissed. Almost all of the men initially selected had illustrious combat records. Many listed up to twenty Civil War engagements and the average for the group was eight.[20]

Included in the first arrivals was Andrew Prince, who had been born in Shenandoah County, Virginia in 1832. He had fought in several battles, including Petersburg, Deep Bottom and Weldon Railroad. Prince had contracted "black scurvy" while working in the water building a pontoon bridge near Petersburg and had never fully recovered. He was dismissed from Fort Dodge in July, 1891, "for tale-bearing and circulating scandalous stories."[21]

Samuel Graham had been raised in Green County, Tennessee. He had served with the First Tennessee Cavalry at Shelbyville, Chickamauga, Mossy Creek, Franklin and Nashville. He was discharged from the home in December, 1890, for "continued violation of the rules, throwing away meat and provisions issued to him, for keeping a woman over sixteen years old at his home, contrary to orders of the commander and for being absent without leave."[22]

John Reed, also one of the first men to make his home at Fort Dodge, had enlisted in L. B. Stopp's Indiana Company of Illinois Volunteers in 1847. An immigrant from Ayrshire, Scotland, Reed had been permanently disabled through prolonged contact with the frozen ground during an engagement near Jalapa, Mexico, in 1848. He was discharged from the home at age 83, "for selling whiskey to other members of the home, using profane language and violating the rules of the home."[23]

George Hyland, born on the Island of Gibraltar, in 1840, had served with the First Ohio Infantry at Buzzard's Roost, Resaca, Altoona, Kenesaw Mountain, Lost Mountain, Peach Tree, Franklin, Nashville, Duck River and Knoxville. He had been disabled by a shell wound in the right side and a bayonet wound in the right leg. He was discharged in 1891, for frequent drunkenness.[24]

Most of the men had small monthy pensions from the government as a result of their war-time service. The average was from four to twelve dollars; however, those who had been severely maimed by the war, such as amputees, had pensions of up to twenty-four dollars.[25]

Shortly after the home was opened, it was decided that dependents of deceased veterans would be admitted on a limited basis. Annie Berry, the widow of Jacob Berry who had died as a result of service contracted tuberculosis, was given a cottage at Fort Dodge during the fall of 1890; however, she quickly married one of the male veterans of the home and thereafter shared her dwelling with him.[26]

Thirty-six men were admitted during the first year of operation. During the first decade, four hundred and twenty-eight men were placed on the roll.[27]

The old soldiers who passed away while in residence had often made previous arrangements to be interred at the post cemetery. The government purchased modest headstones for the graves of all pensioned soldiers; however, relatives were expected to mark the graves of others.[28]

A number of veterans' dependents also found a final resting place at the cemetery. Included was Sopia Spratt, who was perhaps as much a veteran of military life as any man buried there. She had been married to three soldiers during her lifetime and was given a choice burial plot next to James H. "Dog" Kelley. Kelley had gained considerable fame and notoriety as mayor and saloon-keeper at Dodge City. He had been nicknamed "Dog" as a result of his assignment to care for General Custer's hunting dogs during an earlier period when he had served with the United States Seventh Cavalry. Sopia's headstone bore the inscription: "Sopia, wife of Gearhart, Spencer and Spratt. She was faithful to all three soldier boy husbands and is now awaiting reward for faithful service."[29]

By 1900 the animosity so evident toward former Confederate soldiers at the close of the Civil War had subsided and the first former Confederate veteran was admitted. The one thousandth veteran to arrive at Fort Dodge came in 1912. He was Leonard Biggers, the first Negro veteran to be honored with residency at the home. Biggers was a former slave and could not remember when he was born, although he thought his place of birth to be near Summerville, Tennessee. He had enlisted as a private in the United States Fifty-Fifth Colored Infantry near Corinth, Mississippi, in 1863, and had served until the close of the war.[30]

As the years passed, petitions for admission swelled and the home's facilities were increased to accommodate a greater number of veterans. A "sutler's store" was opened which carried a country store line of merchandise. The library which had served the troopers during the military era of the post was maintained and its holdings were slowly increased. A chaplain was engaged to administer to the spiritual needs of the garrison of old soldiers. The old cavalry corrals and buildings were utilized to house a dairy herd for the home's use.[31]

Additional recreational facilities were added for the pleasure of the occupants. Baseball teams from Dodge City and other nearby communities played on the Fort Dodge field to enthusiastic audiences. Indoor and outdoor croquet courts were built and widely used by the soldiers; however, it became necessary to discontinue croquet competition when it became obvious that the game was a chronic source of arguments among participants. Several disputes were settled by assault with mallets and the injuries incurred persuaded the commander that a less potentially lethal source of recreation should be sought.[32]

The streets and residences of the soldier's home reflect a nostalgic observance of the nation's military history. The names of Grant, Custer, Sheridan,

Garfield, Lincoln, Dewey, MacArthur, Nimitz and other figures of the past appear on road signs and building markers.

The old soldiers of the home spend a good portion of their leisure at the post "day room" where billiards, cards and conversation are readily available. In the spring many gather a shovel, hoe, rake and a few packages of seeds and commence gardening, while others take to the banks of the nearby Arkansas River to break the monotony of pseudo-military routine by trying their luck at catfishing.

Visitors willing to engage in conversation are warmly received at the home, where such men as Edward P. Mann enjoy recounting the old days in the army, perhaps for the thousandth time. With a broad smile and eyes still bright at age ninety, Mann will tell those interested what it was like to be with Admiral Dewey in the Philippines during the Spanish-American War:

> I served in the Signal Corps when the whole damned corps had less than a regiment of men. It took us ninety days to get an answer to a letter sent home. For two years we lived on Australian beef, hard tack and American beans and bacon. The damned insects were so bad we had to hang our hats on creosote posts or they would eat them in a matter of hours. You know dysentery killed more men than all the damned bullets and bayonets used.
>
> I remember on the Fourth of July, after the fighting was over, we were in Manila and were looking for some way to celebrate. We only had four artillery pieces at the time, so we held races. While the boys were cheering, four teams of men hitched twelve horses to a field piece, ran the animals a quarter mile and fired the weapon. The winner completed the run and fired in only about ten minutes.[33]

During the post-World War II era, the residency at the home has been held to approximately four hundred members.[34] A modern hospital, an administration building and an intensive care rest home have been added to Fort Dodge facilities.

By 1969, veterans from the Mexican War, Civil War, Indian Wars, Spanish-American War, Philippine Insurrection, Boxer Rebellion, World War I, World War II, Korean War and the Viet Nam War were listed as having been occupants of the post during some stage of the home's service. In retirement, the sentinel to the Cimarron still offered service to the national military establishment; however, the "battles" boasted by the garrison, rather than yesterday's struggle for the plains became yesteryear's American military experience.

NOTES

INTRODUCTION

[1]Henry P. Walker, *The Wagonmasters: High Plains Freighting from the Earliest Days of the Santa Fe Trail Until 1880* (Norman: University of Oklahoma Press, 1965), p. 19.
[2]Walter Prescott Webb, *The Great Plains* (Boston: Ginn and Company, 1939), pp. 115-116.
[3]General Grenville M. Dodge, *The Battle of Atlanta and other Campaigns, Addresses, Etc.* (Council Bluffs, Iowa: The Monarch Printing Co., 1911), p. 73.
[4]Webb, pp. 144-152.
[5]Walker, p. 19.
[6]Ibid., p. 136.
[7]Ibid., p. 27.
[8]Oscar Osburn Winther, *The Transportation Frontier: Trans-Mississippi West, 1865-1890* (New York: Holt Rinehart and Winston, 1964) p. 7.
[9]Walker, p. 27.
[10]Ray Allen Billington, *Westward Expansion: A History of the American Frontier* (New York: The Macmillan Company, 1960), p. 464.
[11]*Senate Executive Documents,* 40 Congress, First Session, Number 13, pp. 111-113.
[12]Ray Allen Billington, *The Far Western Frontier, 1830-1860* (New York: Harper Brothers, 1956), pp. 39-40.
[13]Dodge, pp. 63-66.
[14]Walker D. Wyman, "The Military Phase of Santa Fe Freighting, 1846-1865," *Kansas Historical Quarterly,* I (November, 1932), p. 421.
[15]Robert M. Wright, *Dodge City the Cowboy Capital* (Wichita: The Wichita Eagle Press, 1913), p. 2.
[16]Wyman, p. 421.
[17]*Records of the War Department,* Office of the Adjutant General, Record Group Number 94, Post Returns, Fort Atkinson, Kansas (August, 1850 - September 30, 1853) p. 76.
[18]Stanley Vestal, *The Old Santa Fe Trail* (Boston: Houghton Mifflin Company, 1939), p. 135.
[19]George D. Brewerton, "In the Buffalo Country," *Harper's Magazine,* XXIV (June, 1862), p. 457.
[20]Wyman, p. 415.
[21]*Records of the War Department,* Special Orders 26, 28 and 29, Sixth Military Department (1850).
[22]*Records of the War Department,* Post Returns, Fort Atkinson (April 7, 1853).
[23]*Official Records of the War of the Rebellion,* Series I, Volume 48, p. 1211. Hereafter cited as *Official Records.*
[24]Ibid., pp. 74-75.
[25]*Records of the War Department,* Circular Number 4, Surgeon General's Office, Report on Barracks and Hospitals, with Descriptions of Military Posts, Washington, D. C. (December 5, 1870), p. 301.
[26]*Senate Executive Documents,* 40 Congress, First Session, Number 13, pp. 111-113.
[27]*Records of the War Department,* Letters Sent, 1866-1882, Fort Dodge, Kansas, March 14, 1867. Hereafter cited as Letters Sent.
[28]*Records of the War Department,* Reports and Journals of Scouts and Marches, Fort Dodge, Kansas, 1873-1879, June 10, 1874. Hereafter cited as *Scouts and Marches.*
[29]*Letters Sent,* October 2, 1882.

CHAPTER I

[1]Thomas L. Karnes, "Gilpin's Volunteers on the Santa Fe Trail," *Kansas Historical Quarterly,* XXX (Spring, 1964), p. 1.
[2]Ibid., p. 3
[3]Ibid., p. 13.
[4]Ibid., pp. 13-14.

CHAPTER I continued

[5]*Kansas Weekly Herald* (Leavenworth), June 14, 1856, p. 2.

[6]*Kansas Weekly Herald,* March 2, 1855, p. 1. *Weekly Osage Chronicle* (Burlingame), August 5, 1865, p. 1. Newspapers such as the pro-slavery *Kansas Weekly Herald,* and the abolitionist *Weekly Osage Chronicle* increased public tension over the slavery issue by publishing acid editorials charging the opposition with maintaining outlaw bands which preyed on the citizenry of Kansas. The editorial contest was not resolved until Kansas entered the Union as a free state in 1861.

[7]*Kansas Weekly Herald,* June 14, 1856, p. 2.

[8]Albert Castel, *A Frontier State At War: Kansas 1861-1865* (Ithaca: Cornell University Press, 1958), pp. 17-36.

[9]*Governor's Papers,* Archives, Kansas State Historical Society, Topeka, Joel K. Goodwin to Acting Territorial Governor Hugh S. Walsh, October 18, 1858. Hereafter cited as *Governor's Papers.*

[10]*Governor's Papers,* Governor James W. Denver to A. P. Wilson, June 4, 1858.

[11]*Records of the War Department,* Reports and Journals of Scouts and Marches, 1873-1879, Fort Dodge, Kansas, August 31, 1874. Hereafter cited as *Scouts and Marches. Junction City Union* (Junction City), January 30, 1875, p. 2. There are numerous reports of "bushwhacking" or outlawry by roving bands of whites included in the military records of Fort Dodge, Kansas and by several Kansas newspapers until the mid-1870's. These groups committed attacks on settlements with alarming regularity throughout the post-Civil War period. Many of the forays extended well into the Indian Territory, where horses were stolen from many of the tribes and removed to Kansas for sale.

[12]Noble L. Prentis, *A History of Kansas* (Topeka: Caroline Prentis, 1909), p. 143.

[13]William F. Zornow, *Kansas: A History of the Jayhawk State* (Norman: University of Oklahoma Press, 1959), p. 108.

[14]Castel, pp. 54-55.

[15]Prentis, pp. 147-148.

[16]Castel, p. 157.

[17]*Governor's Papers,* W. P. Dole, Commissioner of Indian Affairs to Governor Thomas Carney, October 25, 1863.

[18]*Official Records of the War of the Rebellion,* Series I Volume XXII, pp. 333-334. Hereafter cited as *Official Records.*

[19]*Smoky Hill and Republican Union* (Junction City), June 25, 1864, p. 1. George B. Grinnell, *The Fighting Cheyennes* (New York: Charles Scribner's Sons, 1915), p. 114.

[20]Paul I. Wellman, *Death on the Prairie* (New York: Macmillan Company, 1954), p. 96.

[21]Robert W. Frazer, *Forts of the West* (Norman: University of Oklahoma Press, 1965), p. 55.

[22]*Smoky Hill and Republican Union,* April 4, 1862, p. 3.

[23]*Western Journal of Commerce* (St. Louis), July 11, 1863, p. 1.

[24]*Smoky Hill and Republican Union,* June 25, 1864, p. 1.

[25]*Smoky Hill and Republican Union,* July 21, 1862, p. 1.

[26]Ibid., July 23, 1864, p. 1.

[27]Oscar Osburn Winther, *The Transportation Frontier Trans-Mississippi West, 1865-1890* (New York: Holt, Rinehart and Winston, 1964), p. 12.

[28]Ralph K. Andrist, *The Long Death: The Last Days of the Plains Indian* (New York: The Macmillan Company, 1964), pp. 76-77.

[29]Marvin H. Garfield, "Defense of the Kansas Frontier, 1864-1865," *Kansas Historical Quarterly,* I (February, 1932), p. 141.

[30]Andrist, p. 78.

[31]*Western Journal of Commerce,* July 9, 1864, p. 2.

[32]*Western Journal of Commerce,* July 30, 1864, p. 1.

[33]*Smoky Hill and Republican Union,* October 8, 1864, p. 1.

[34]Ibid.

[35]*Weekly Osage Chronicle,* August 27, 1864, p. 1.

[36]Ibid.

[37]Andrist, pp. 85-88.

[38]Garfield, "Defense of the Kansas Frontier, 1864-1865," p. 146.

[39]Andrist, p. 91

[40]Ibid., pp. 89-90.

CHAPTER I continued

[41]*Smoky Hill and Republican Union,* November 12, 1864, p. 1.
[42]Garfield, "Defense of the Kansas Frontier, 1864-1865," p. 145.
[43]Ibid.
[44]*Western Journal of Commerce,* October 21, 1865, p. 1.
[45]Marvin Garfield, "The Military Post as a Factor in the Frontier Defense of Kansas, 1865-1869," *Kansas Historical Quarterly,* I (November, 1931), p. 55.
[46]Ibid., p. 54.
[47]Garfield, "Defense of Kansas Frontier," p. 146.
[48]General Grenville M. Dodge, *The Battle of Atlanta and other Campaigns, Addresses, Etc.* (Council Bluffs, Iowa: The Monarch Printing Company, 1911), Introduction.
[49]Ibid., p. 63.
[50]Ibid., p. 64.
[51]Ibid., p. 63.
[52]Ibid.
[53]Ibid., p. 64.
[54]Ibid., 64.
[55]Ibid., p. 67.
[56]*Western Journal of Commerce,* March 25, 1865, p. 1.
[57]Dodge, p. 72.
[58]Ibid., p. 77.
[59]*Official Records,* Series I, Volume 48, pp. 862-863.
[60]Ibid., p. 863.
[61]Ibid., pp. 923-924.
[62]Ibid., p. 961.
[63]Ibid., p. 923.
[64]Ibid., p. 1186.
[65]Ibid., p. 1186.
[66]Ibid., p. 1204.
[67]Ibid.
[68]Ibid., p. 1224.
[69]Ibid., pp. 74-75.
[70]*Records of the War Department,* Circular Number Four, Surgeon General's Office, Report on Barracks and Hospitals, with Descriptions of Military Posts, Washington, D. C. (December 5, 1870), p. 301. Hereafter cited as *Surgeon General's Office.*
[71]Ibid.
[72]*Official Records,* p. 54.
[73]Ibid.
[74]Dodge, p. 80.
[75]Ibid.
[76]Ibid.
[77]Ibid., p. 83.
[78]Ibid.
[79]*Official Records,* Series I, Volume 28, pp. 308-309.
[80]Dodge, pp. 82-83.
[81]Ibid.
[82]Ibid.
[83]Ibid.
[84]*Treaty of the Little Arkansas,* Official Copy, Archives, Kansas State Historical Society, Topeka, Kansas.
[85]Ray Allen Billington, *Westward Expansion: A History of the American Frontier* (New York: The Macmillan Company, 1960), pp. 664-665.
[86]*Junction City Union,* September 30, 1865, p. 1.
[87]Dodge, pp. 106-107.
[88]Ibid., p. 102.
[89]*Records of the War Department,* General Order Number 22, Headquarters, Department of the Missouri, September 17, 1865.
[90]Ibid., Number 33, October 26, 1865.
[91]Garfield, "Defense of Kansas Frontier," p. 150.
[92]Andrist, p. 153.

CHAPTER II

[1]*Records of the War Department,* Circular Number 4, Surgeon General's Office, Report On Barracks and Hospitals, with Descriptions of Military Posts, Washington, D. C., (December 5, 1870), p. 301. Hereafter cited as *Surgeon General's Office.*
[2]Ibid., Circular Number 8 (May 1, 1875), p. 254.
[3]*Official Records of the War of the Rebellion,* Series I, Volume 48, p. 1211.
[4]*Surgeon General's Office,* Circular Number 4, p. 301.
[5]Ibid.
[6]Ibid.
[7]Richard Irving Dodge, *Plains of the Great West* (New York: Archer House, Inc., 1959), p. 22.
[8]*Surgeon General's Office,* Number 8, pp. 256-257.
[9]*Surgeon General's Office,* Number 4, p. 303.
[10]Theodore Davis, "Winter on the Plains," *Harper's Magazine,* XXXIX (June, 1869), p. 24.
[11]Letter, General Grenville M. Dodge to Joseph B. Thoburn (October 24, 1910), Archives, *Kansas State Historical Society,* Topeka, Kansas.
[12]*Records of the War Department,* Letters Sent, 1866-1882, Fort Dodge, Kansas, March 14, 1867. Hereafter cited as *Letters Sent.*
Kate W. Krumery, *Saga of the Sawlog* (Denver: Big Mountain Press, 1965), p. 14.
[13]*Surgeon General's Office,* Number 4, p. 303.
[14]*Letters Sent,* June 7, 1866.
[15]Ibid., November 24, 1866.
[16]Ibid., June 20, 1866.
[17]Ibid., November 24, 1866.
[18]Theodore Weichselbaum, "Statement of Theodore Weichselbaum of Ogden, Riley County, July 17, 1908," *Kansas Historical Quarterly,* XI (1909-1910), pp. 561-571.
[19]*Letters Sent,* August 25, 1866.
[20]Ibid.
[21]*Surgeon General's Office,* Number 4, p. 301.
[22]*Letters Sent,* April 7, 1866.
[23]*Records of the War Department,* Post Returns, Fort Dodge, Kansas 1866-1882 (December 1, 1866). Hereafter cited as *Post Returns.*
[24]*Letters Sent,* March 16, 1866.
[25]Ibid., November 5, 1866.
[26]Ibid., December 21, 1866.
[27]Ibid., April 22, 1866.
[28]Ibid., August 9, 1866.
[29]Ibid., March 8, 1866.
[30]Drawing 189, Kansas, 8-3, Military Reservations, Fort Dodge, Kansas, Archives, *Kansas State Historical Society,* Topeka, Kansas.
[31]*Letters Sent,* May 26, 1866.
[32]*Records of the War Department,* Special Orders, Fort Dodge, Kansas, 1866-1882. Hereafter cited as *Special Orders.*
[33]Ibid., Number 18, September 13, 1867.
[34]*Letters Sent,* January 13, 1867.
[35]Ibid.
[36]*Senate Executive Documents,* 40 Congress, First Session, Number 11, p. 41.
[37]Ibid., Number 13, pp. 49-51.
[38]Ibid., pp. 1-6.
[39]*Records of the War Department,* Consolidated Quartermaster Records, 1865-1882, Fort Dodge, Kansas, October 30, 1866. Hereafter cited as *Quartermaster Records.*
[40]Ibid.
[41]*Post Returns,* November, 1867.
[42]*Quartermaster Records,* October 30, 1867.
[43]*Surgeon General's Office,* Number 8, pp. 254-255. The dimensions of all of the permanent stone buildings erected during 1866 and 1867, with the exception of the commanding officer's quarters, were almost identical. Although slight variations were necessary due to the anticipated use of the structures, all of the buildings were approximately one hundred thirty feet long and thirty feet wide.

CHAPTER II continued

[44]Ibid.
[45]Ibid.
[46]*Quartermaster Records,* October 30, 1867.
[47]Ibid.
[48]Ibid.
[49]*Surgeon General's Office,* Number 4, p. 303.
[50]Ibid., p. 302.
[51]Ibid., pp. 302-303.
[52]*Quartermaster Records,* August 14, 1866.
[53]*Post Returns,* November, 1867.
[54]*Quartermaster Records,* May 1, 1866.
[55]*Letters Sent,* September 10, 1867. Ibid., September 20, 1867, R. W. Fish to Governor Crawford. This letter notes that seven hundred Spencer rifles, one hundred and seventy thousand rounds of ammunition and a "large number" of Remington revolvers with ammunition were lost during the attack.
[56]Ibid., September 7, 1867. Ibid., October 28, 1867.
[57]*Records of the War Department,* Consolidated Medical Records, Weekly Report of Sick and Wounded, Fort Dodge, Kansas, July 11, 1867, August 3, 1867. Hereafter cited as *Medical Records.*
[58]*Surgeon General's Office,* Number 4, p. 303.
[59]*Letters Sent,* February 22, 1866.
[60]Ibid., March 5, 1866.
[61]Ibid., October 1, 1866.
[62]Ibid.
[63]Ibid., October 20, 1866.
[64]Leo E. Oliva, *Soldiers on the Santa Fe Trail, 1829-1880* (Norman: University of Oklahoma Press, 1967), pp. 182-183.
[65]Ibid.
[66]*Senate Executive Documents,* Number 13, p. 81.
[67]*Letters Sent,* February 13, 1867.
[68]*Junction City Union,* August 3, 1866, p. 2. *Western Osage Chronicle,* September 29, 1866, p. 1.
[69]William E. Unrau, "Indian Agent vs the Army: Some Background Notes on the Kiowa-Comanche Treaty of 1865," *Kansas Historical Quarterly,* XXX (Summer, 1964), pp. 146-147.
[70]Samuel J. Crawford, *Kansas in the Sixties* (Chicago: A. C. McClurg and Company, 1911), pp. 231-232.
[71]*Junction City Union,* August 3, 1867, p. 1.
[72]*Letters Sent,* March 19, 1867.
[73]Ibid., March 5, 1867.
[74]Ibid., March 2, 1867.
[75]*Junction City Union,* December 19, 1866, p. 1.
[76]Ibid.
[77]Unrau, p. 145.
[78]Ibid.
[79]*Letters Sent,* February 13, 1867.
[80]Ibid., March 24, 1867.
[81]Ralph K. Andrist, *The Long Death* (New York: Macmillan, 1964), pp. 174-175. Henry M. Stanley, *My Early Travels and Adventures in America and Asia* (London: Sampson Low, Marston and Company, 1895), I, pp. 64-78.
[82]*Letters Sent,* February 13, 1867. Ibid., March 19, 1867. Ibid., March 24, 1867.
[83]Ibid., March 19, 1867.
[84]Ibid., February 24, 1867.
[85]Ibid., February 13, 1867.
[86]Ibid., February 10, 1867.
[87]Ibid., March 14, 1867.
[88]Ibid., March 2, 1867.
[89]Ibid., March 3, 1867.

CHAPTER II continued

[90]*Records of the War Department,* General Orders, Number 29, Headquarters, Department of the Missouri, Fort Leavenworth, Kansas, Feburary 25, 1867. Hereafter cited as *Gereral Orders.*
[91]*Special Orders,* Number 56, May 8, 1867.
[92]*Records of the War Department,* General Field Orders, Number 1, Headquarters, Department of the Missouri, March 26, 1867. Hereafter cited as *General Field Orders.*
[93]Oliva, p. 186.
[94]*Senate Executive Documents,* Number 13, p. 81.
[95]Theodore R. Lewis, "A Summer on the Plains," *Harper's Magazine,* XXXVI (May, 1868), p. 295.
[96]*Junction City Union,* April 20, 1867, p. 1.
[97]Stanley, pp. 30-31.
[98]*Senate Executive Documents,* Number 13, p. 84.
[99]Lewis, p. 295.
[100]*Senate Executive Documents,* Number 13, p. 85.
[101]Stanley, pp. 45-46.
[102]*Senate Executive Documents,* Number 13, pp. 85-86.
[103]Stanley, p. 40.
[104]*Letters Sent,* April 17, 1867.
[105]Stanley, pp. 47-48.
[106]Ibid., pp. 48-49.
[107]*Letters Sent,* April 19, 1867.
[108]Stanley, p. 49.
[109]Lewis, p. 297.
[110]Stanley, pp. 62-78.
[111]Ibid., pp. 64-65.
[112]Lewis, p. 297.
[113]*Junction City Union,* July 28, 1867, p. 1.
[114]Lewis, p. 298.
[115]Andrist, p. 144.
[116]*Letters Sent,* June 8, 1867.
[117]Ibid.
[118]Ibid., June 12, 1867.
[119]Ibid.
[120]Ibid., July 3, 1867.
[121]Lewis, p. 298.
[122]Ibid., June 14, 1867.
[123]Ibid., June 18, 1867.
[124]Ibid.
[125]*Junction City Union,* June 29, 1867, p. 1.
[126]Ibid.
[127]Ibid.
[128]Ibid.
[129]Ibid., July 22, 1867, p. 1.
[130]*Letters Sent,* October 5, 1867.
[131]Ibid., November 19, 1867.
[132]Ibid.
[133]Ibid.
[134]Ibid.
[135]Ibid.
[136]Ibid.
[137]*Dodge City Daily Globe* (Dodge City), December 24, 1934, p. 1.
[138]Ibid.
[139]*Junction City Union,* May 18, 1867, p. 1. Ibid, July 22, 1867, p. 1.
[140]*Western Osage Chronicle,* September 28, 1867, p. 3.
[141]Andrist, p. 146.
[142]*Western Osage Chronicle,* September 28, 1867, p. 3.

CHAPTER II continued

[143]Crawford, p. 265.
[144]Ibid., pp. 272-274.
[145]Ibid., pp. 273-274.
[146]Ibid., pp. 275-276.
[147]Ibid., p. 275.
[148]Ibid., pp. 276-277.
[149]Andrist, p. 146.
[150]Carl C. Rister, *Border Command: General Phil Sheridan in the West* (Norman: University of Oklahoma Press, 1944), p. 59.
[151]*Treaty of Medicine Lodge,* Official Copy, Archives, Kansas State Historical Society, Topeka, Kansas.
[152]Ibid.
[153]Andrist, p. 146.
[154]William E. Connelley, "The Treaty Held at Medicine Lodge," *Kansas Historical Collections,* XVII (1926-28), pp. 601-604.

CHAPTER III

[1]*Records of the War Department,* Circular Number 4, Surgeon General's Office, Report on Barracks and Hospitals, with Descriptions of Military Posts, Washington, D. C., (December 5, 1870), p. 301. Hereafter cited as *Surgeon General's Office.*
[2]Ibid., Number 8, p. 254.
[3]Ibid., Number 4, p. 302.
[4]Ibid., Number 8, p. 254.
[5]*Records of the War Department,* Letters Sent, 1866-1882, Fort Dodge, Kansas, October 2, 1877. Hereafter cited as *Letters Sent.*
[6]*Records of the War Department,* Consolidated Quartermaster Records, 1865-1882, Fort Dodge, Kansas, May 26, 1875. Hereafter cited as *Quartermaster Records.*
[7]*Letters Sent,* May 10, 1876.
[8]*Records of the War Department,* Consolidated Medical Records, Weekly Report of Sick and Wounded, Fort Dodge, Kansas, May 1, 1875. Hereafter cited as *Medical Records.*
[9]Brigadier General George A. Forsyth, *The Story of the Soldier* (New York: D. Appleton and Company, 1905), p. 54.
[10]Ibid.
[11]*Dodge City Times* (Dodge City), October 28, 1877, p. 3.
[12]Forsyth, pp. 95-96. The clothing allotment given to the enlisted man on his entry into the army consisted of one overcoat, two uniform dress coats, three woolen blouses, three canvas fatigue blouses, seven pairs of uniform trousers, seven pairs of jersey trousers, three pairs of canvas fatigue trousers, three pairs of overalls, seven blue woolen shirts, nine undershirts, nine pair of underpants, thirty-six linen collars, twelve pairs of cotton socks, twelve pairs of woolen socks, nine pairs of shoes for infantry and two pairs of boots and five pairs of shoes for cavalry, four fatigue caps, three campaign hats, two helmets, two woolen blankets, twenty-four pairs gloves and three pairs of suspenders.
[13]*Letters Sent,* July 6, 1871.
[14]*Medical Records,* January 11, 1880.
[15]*Records of the War Department,* Headquarters, Department of the Missouri, Special Orders, Number 155, September 9, 1876. Hereafter cited as *Special Orders.*
[16]*Medical Records,* March 18, 1874.
[17]Ibid.
[18]*Letters Sent,* July 3, 1879.
[19]*Surgeon General's Office,* Number 4, p. 303.
[20]*Special Orders,* Number 99, August 1, 1881.
[21]*Medical Records,* January 1, 1875.
[22]*Letters Sent,* April 7, 1871.

CHAPTER III continued

[23]*Quartermaster Records,* October 2, 1873.
[24]*Special Orders,* Number 59, June 30, 1877. Ibid., Number 61, July 2, 1877.
[25]*Records of the War Department,* Military Division of the Missouri, Contract Number 2776, July 9, 1873.
[26]*Special Orders,* Number 61, July 2, 1877.
[27]*Letters Sent,* April 1, 1868.
[28]Ibid.
[29]Ibid.
[30]Ibid., May 19, 1879. Ibid., July 30, 1879.
[31]*Special Orders,* Number 96, July 18, 1879.
[32]Ibid., Number 37, April 30, 1881.
[33]Ibid., Number 100, July 1, 1871.
[34]Ibid., Number 149, December 1, 1878.
[35]Ibid., Number 30, April 19, 1881.
[36]Ibid., Number 179, December 6, 1873.
[37]*Letters Sent,* March 25, 1873.
[38]*Special Orders,* Number 34, May 25, 1881.
[39]*Letters Sent,* May 3, 1870.
[40]Ibid., September 19, 1871.
[41]*Records of the War Department,* Reports and Journals of Scouts and Marches, Fort Dodge, Kansas, 1873-1878, July 14, 1873. Hereafter cited as *Scouts and Marches.*
[42]*Letters Sent,* May 30, 1874.
[43]*Special Orders,* Number 140, October 8, 1881.
[44]Ibid., Number 46, May 8, 1877. Ibid., Number 37, March 16, 1878.
[45]*Medical Records,* January 1, 1875.
[46]*Special Orders,* Number 46, May 8, 1877.
[47]*Letters Sent,* November 8, 1871.
[48]*Scouts and Marches,* February 24, 1868.
[49]*Special Orders,* Number 198, November 7, 1868.
[50]*Records of the War Department,* Post Returns, Fort Dodge, Kansas 1866-1882, October, 1872. Hereafter cited as *Post Returns.*
[51]*Dodge City Times,* March 1, 1878, p. 1.
[52]*Letters Sent,* July 22, 1876.
[53]*Dodge City Times,* March 27, 1878, p. 2.
[54]Ibid., September 22, 1878, p. 2.
[55]*Records of the War Department,* Letters Sent, August 30, 1864-April 2, 1876, Fort Harker, Kansas, September 14, 1866.
[56]*Letters Sent,* April 18, 1868, January 5, 1870.
[57]*Special Orders,* Number 129, September 23, 1881.
[58]*Letters Sent,* March 1, 1868.
[59]Ibid.
[60]Ibid.
[61]Ibid.
[62]Ibid., April 13, 1873.
[63]Ibid.
[64]*Scouts and Marches,* June 10, 1874.
[65]Special Orders, Number 10, January 15, 1876. Ibid., Number 12, January 18, 1876.
[66]*Scouts and Marches,* July 28, 1873.
[67]*Letters Sent,* November 10, 1868.
[68]Ibid., September 23, 1874.
[69]*Scouts and Marches,* July 28, 1873.
[70]*Special Orders,* Number 30, March 2, 1878.
[71]*Letters Sent,* September 15, 1867.
[72]*Medical Records,* January 1, 1875.
[73]*Letters Sent,* September 15, 1867.
[74]Robert M. Wright, *Dodge City the Cowboy Capital* (Wichita: The Wichita Eagle Press, 1913), p. 46.
[75]*Letters Sent,* September 15, 1867.

CHAPTER III continued

[76]*Special Orders,* Number 14, January 1, 1879.
[77]*Post Returns,* November, 1868, June, 1873.
[78]*Special Orders,* Number 201, November 11, 1868.
[79]Ibid.
[80]*Scouts and Marches,* July 28, 1873. *Letters Sent,* August 28, 1867, November 18, 1868.
[81]*Senate Executive Documents,* 40 Congress, First Session, Number 13, p. 96. Leo E. Oliva, *Soldiers on the Santa Fe Trail, 1829-1880* (Norman: University of Oklahoma Press, 1967), p. 185.
[82]*Letters Sent,* April 3, 1869, April 16, 1869.
[83]*Special Orders,* Number 52, March 18, 1869.
[84]Ibid., November 6, 1868.
[85]Ibid., Number 131, October 19, 1867. Ibid., Number 118, July 13, 1874.
[86]*Letters Sent,* March 18, 1871.
[87]*Special Orders,* Number 140, August 20, 1868.
[88]*Scouts and Marches,* August 23, 1868.
[89]*Letters Sent,* January 24, 1868.
[90]Ibid.
[91]Ibid., September 15, 1867.
[92]Ibid., June 18, 1872.
[93]Ibid., July 1, 1872.
[94]Ibid., September 3, 1872, January 1, 1874.
[95]*Special Orders,* Number 98, June 11, 1876.
[96]Ibid., Number 15, January 27, 1878.
[97]*Letters Sent,* January 7, 1879, January 26, 1879.
[98]*Dodge City Times,* August 8, 1881, p. 1.
[99]Gilbert C. Fite, "The United States Army and Relief to Pioneer Settlers, 1874-1875," *Journal of the West,* VI (January, 1967), pp. 99-107.
[100]*Dodge City Times,* July 28, 1877.
[101]*Medical Records,* August 30, 1877.
[102]*Letters Sent,* April 1, 1868.
[103]Ibid.
[104]*Dodge City Times,* July 28, 1877, May 28, 1882.
[105]*Letters Sent,* September 10, 1876.
[106]Ibid., November 18, 1868.
[107]Ibid., November 28, 1868.
[108]Ibid., May 27, 1872.
[109]Ibid., November 3, 1870.
[110]Ibid., August 29, 1872.
[111]Ibid., June 15, 1872.
[112]Wright, p. 333.
[113]*Dodge City Times,* February 12, 1881, p. 1.
[114]*Letters Sent,* May 27, 1872.
[115]Richard Irving Dodge, *Plains of the Great West* (New York: Archer House Inc., 1959), p. 67.
[116]Wright, pp. 83-85.
[117]*Letters Sent,* May 26, 1868.
[118]*Special Orders,* Number 58, March 21, 1869.
[119]*Letters Sent,* July 6, 1871.
[120]Ibid., October 14, 1873.
[121]*Quartermaster Records,* September 24, 1875. After the laundresses were moved from the dugouts in 1872, they were housed in several vacant frame buildings until four sets of permanent quarters were completed in 1875.
[122]*Letters Sent,* June 15, 1872.
[123]*Special Orders,* Number 24, February 1, 1869.
[124]*Letters Sent,* May 26, 1869.
[125]*Special Orders,* Number 2, March 11, 1881. Number 3, March 12, 1881, Number 4, March 12, 1881, Number 14, March 28, 1881, Number 121, September 8, 1881, Number 172, November 28, 1881.

CHAPTER III continued

[126]*Letters Sent,* November 8, 1871, November 11, 1871, March 4, 1873.
[127]*Special Orders,* Number 171, October 5, 1868.
[128]*Letters Sent,* March 4, 1873.
[129]Ibid.
[130]Ibid., March 7, 1868.
[131]Ibid., November 9, 1868.
[132]Ibid., May 5, 1868.
[133]*Special Orders,* Number 2, January 3, 1869.
[134]*Letters Sent,* May 5, 1869.
[135]Ibid., November 26, 1871.
[136]*Surgeon General's Office,* Number 8, p. 254.
[137]*Letters Sent,* August 7, 1871.
[138]Ibid., December 10, 1874.
[139]*Special Orders,* Number 2, March 12, 1881, Ibid., Number 4, March 15, 1881.
[140]Ibid., Number 14, March 28, 1881.
[141]Ibid., Number 4, March 15, 1881.
[142]*Post Returns,* April, 1866, March, 1882.
[143]Ibid., January, 1867, January, 1875.
[144]*Letters Sent,* January 16, 1886. The Fort Dodge records include numerous letters and telegrams from the forts along the Santa Fe and Smoky Hill Routes asking for help in apprehending deserters. The frequency of these requests for assistance indicate that heavy desertion was experienced by all of the posts in Western Kansas.
[145]*Letters Sent,* May 21, 1876.
[146]Ibid., April 16, 1866, February 25, 1869.
[147]Don Rickey, Jr., *Forty Miles a Day on Beans and Hay: The Enlisted Soldier Fighting the Indian Wars* (Norman: University of Oklahoma Press, 1963), p. 153.
[148]Ibid., p. 149.
[149]Theodore R. Lewis, "A Summer on the Plains," *Harper's Magazine,* XXXVI (May, 1868), p. 298.
[150]*Letters Sent,* November 24, 1873.
[151]Ibid.
[152]Ibid., January 11, 1872, April 14, 1878.
[153]*Special Orders,* Number 1, March 24, 1881.
[154]*Letters Sent,* May 21, 1876.
[155]Ibid., May 28, 1869.
[156]*Medical Records,* October 30, 1865, October 2, 1882. The surgeons of Fort Dodge kept a monthly record of the various illnesses contacted by the soldiers throughout the post hospital's years of service. In addition to the sickcall rolls, a brief medical history and critique of the fort's military life was written each year and forwarded to the Office of the Surgeon General, Washington, D. C.
[157]Ibid., January 5, 1873, January 1, 1875.
[158]*Special Orders,* Number 116, July 1, 1874.
[159]*Medical Records,* January 1, 1875.
[160]Ibid., June 30, 1867.
[161]Dodge, p. 95.
[162]Ibid., p. 96.
[163]*Medical Records,* October 30, 1868, March 18, 1874.
[164]Ibid., June 27, 1867.
[165]Ibid., June 30, 1865, October 2, 1882.
[166]Dodge, p. 39.
[167]*Letters Sent,* February 3, 1874, June 28, 1876.
[168]*Medical Records,* January 5, 1873, June 17, 1879.
[169]Ibid., May 30, 1867, November 30, 1868, October 30, 1874, March 30, 1875.
[170]Ibid., January 5, 1875.
[171]Ibid., September 25, 1867.
[172]Ibid., January 1, 1875.
[173]Ibid., June 30, 1867, May 30, 1868.
[174]Ibid., September 25, 1867.

CHAPTER III continued

[175]Dodge, p. 39.
[176]*Dodge City Times,* October 5, 1878, p. 1.
[177]*Medical Records,* December 1, 1875.
[178]*Post Returns,* February 1, 1879.
[179]*Medical Records,* January 1, 1875.
[180]*Post Returns,* September 24, 1880.
[181]*Dodge City Times,* June 1, 1877, p. 1, November 1, 1879, p. 2.
[182]*Special Orders,* Number 29, April 18, 1881.
[183]Ibid., Number 130, September 24, 1881.
[184]Ibid., Number 15, March 28, 1881.
[185]*Letters Sent,* February 21, 1869.
[186]*Quartermaster Records,* July 19, 1878.
[187]Ibid.

CHAPTER IV

[1]*Junction City Union* (Junction City), October 17, 1868, p. 3.
[2]Ralph K. Andrist, *The Long Death* (New York: Macmillan, 1964), p. 154.
[3]Ibid.
[4]*Records of the War Department,* Letters Sent, 1866-1882, Fort Dodge, Kansas, January 16, 1868. Hereafter cited as *Letters Sent.*
[5]Ibid., March 21, 1868.
[6]*Weekly Osage Chronicle* (Burlingame), February 15, 1868, p. 1.
[7]*Governor's Papers,* Archives, Kansas State Historical Society, Topeka, A. A. Moore to Governor Crawford, June 6, 1868. Hereafter cited as *Governor's Papers.*
[8]Ibid., S. C. True to Governor Crawford, April 10, 1868.
[9]Ibid., William C. Vassar to Governor Crawford, June 14, 1868.
[10]*Weekly Osage Chronicle,* August 29, 1868, p. 1.
[11]Marvin Garfield, "Defense of the Kansas Frontier, 1864-1865," *Kansas Historical Quarterly,* I (February, 1932), p. 451.
[12]*Letters Sent,* September 24, 1868.
[13]Lieutenant General Philip H. Sheridan, Commander, *Records of Engagements with Hostile Indians within the Military Division of the Missouri from 1868 to 1882,* Compiled from Official Records, Headquarters, Military Division of the Missouri, Chicago, 1882.
[14]*Letters Sent,* September 24, 1868.
[15]Garfield, p. 458.
[16]Andrist, p. 149.
[17]Sheridan, pp. 13-14.
[18]Andrist, p. 150.
[19]Sheridan, p. 13-14.
[20]*House Executive Documents,* 40 Congress, 3 Session, Number 1, (Serial 1367), p. 14.
[21]*Records of the War Department,* Consolidated Medical Records, Weekly Report of Sick and Wounded, Fort Dodge, Kansas, September 30, 1868. Hereafter cited as Medical Records.
[22]Robert M. Wright, *Dodge City the Cowboy Capital* (Wichita: The Wichita Eagle Press, 1913), p. 116.
[23]*House Executive Documents,* 40 Congress 3 Session, Number 1 (Serial 1367), p. 14.
[24]*Governor's Papers,* General Sheridan to Governor Crawford, October 9, 1868.
[25]Sheridan, p. 17.
[26]*House Executive Documents,* Number 1, pp. 16-17.
[27]*House Executive Documents,* 41 Congress, 2 Session, Report of Secretary of War (Serial 1412), p. 45.
[28]A. L. Runyon, "A. L. Runyon's Letters from the Nineteenth Kansas Regiment," *Kansas Historical Quarterly,* IX (February, 1949), pp. 58-75.
[29]*House Executive Documents,* Secretary of War, p. 45.

CHAPTER IV continued

[30]Ibid.
[31]Runyon, pp. 62-63.
[32]Ibid.
[33]Horace L. Moore, "The Nineteenth Kansas Cavalry," *Kansas Historical Collections,* VI (1897-1900), pp. 39-40.
[34]*House Executive Documents,* Secretary of War, p. 47.
[35]Lonnie J. White, "Winter Campaigning with Sheridan and Custer: The Expedition of the 19th Kansas Volunteer Cavalry": *Journal of the West,* VI (January, 1967), p. 76.
[36]*House Executive Documents,* Secretary of War, p. 46.
[37]Andrist, pp. 157-158.
[38]*Letters Sent,* November 27, 1868.
[39]*House Executive Documents,* Secretary of War, p. 46.
[40]*Letters Sent,* November 30, 1868.
[41]*House Executive Documents,* Secretary of War, p. 48.
[42]Garfield, p. 465.
[43]*Junction City Union,* January 9, 1869, p. 2.
[44]Ibid.
[45]*Medical Records,* January 30, 1869.
[46]*House Executive Documents,* Secretary of War, p. 47.
[47]Moore, p. 42-43.
[48]Garfield, p. 466.
[49]*House Executive Documents,* Secretary of War, p. 49.
[50]Ibid.
[51]Sheridan, pp. 19-20.
[52]Andrist, p. 166.
[53]Moore, p. 46.
[54]Flora Seymour, *Indian Agents of the Old Frontier* (New York: Macmillan, 1941), p. 60.
[55]Colonel George Ward Nichols, "The Indian: What We Should Do With Him," *Harper's Magazine,* XV (May, 1870), pp. 723-739.
[56]Seymour, p. 60.
[57]Ibid., p. 69.
[58]*Junction City Union,* June 18, 1879, p. 3.
[59]Andrist, p. 179.
[60]Ibid.
[61]*House Executive Documents,* 42 Congress, 3 Session, Number 1 (Serial 1558), p. 47.
[62]*Junction City Union,* November 21, 1873, p. 4.
[63]*Letters Sent,* October 18, 1873.
[64]Andrist, p. 183.
[65]*Letters Sent,* July 21, 1874.
[66]*Records of the War Department,* Telegrams Received, Fort Dodge, Kansas, 1874. Hereafter cited as *Telegrams Received. Senate Executive Documents,* 40th Congress, 1st Session, Number 13, p. 53. *Letters Sent,* November 6, 1868, March 27, 1869, October 31, 1870, November 3, 1870, December 10, 1870, May 28, 1872, May 29, 1872.
[67]Andrist, p. 184.
[68]C. E. Campbell, "Down Among the Red Men," *Kansas Historical Collections* XVII (1926-1928), p. 633.
[69]Ibid., p. 635.
[70]Andrist, p. 186.
[71]*Governor's Papers,* Telegrams, Charles Rath to Governor Osborn, July 8, 1874.
[72]Andrist, pp. 185-187.
[73]*Governor's Papers,* Telegrams Charles Rath to Governor Osborn, July 19, 1874.
[74]*Telegrams Received,* July 7, 1874.
[75]*Letters Sent,* July 7, 1874.
[76]*Telegrams Received,* July 7, 1874.
[77]Ibid., July 9, 1874.
[78]*Governor's Papers,* Telegrams, R. W. Wright to Governor Osborn, July 9, 1874.
[79]Ibid., General Pope to Governor Osborn, July 8, 1874.
[80]Andrist, p. 189.

CHAPTER IV continued

[81]*Letters Sent,* October 27, 1873.
[82]Ibid., June 20, 1874.
[83]*Telegrams Received,* June 25, 1874.
[84]*Letters Sent,* July 2, 1874.
[85]Ibid., September 1, 1874.
[86]*Governor's Papers,* Telegrams, Governor Osborn to W. A. Phillips, September 19, 1874.
[87]*Telegrams Received,* September 17, 1874.
[88]Andrist, p. 189.
[89]*Governor's Papers,* Telegrams, Governor Osborn to President Grant, July 21, 1874. Ibid., Letters, Levi P. Suchy, Secretary to the President to Governor Osborn, August 27, 1874.
[90]*Telegrams Received,* August 11, 1874.
[91]*Letters Sent,* August 11, 1874.
[92]Ibid., September 9, 1874, September 17, 1874.
[93]Andrist, p. 192.
[94]*Telegrams Received,* August 27, 1874.
[95]*Letters Sent,* August 31, 1874.
[96]*Junction City Union,* September 26, 1874.
[97]Andrist, pp. 193-195.
[98]*Letters Sent,* November 26, 1874.
[99]Ibid., November 28, 1874.
[100]Ibid.
[101]*Medical Records,* January 5, 1875, January 30, 1875
[102]*Letters Sent,* November 25, 1875.
[103]*Junction City Union,* January 30, 1875, p. 2
[104]Campbell, p. 652.
[105]Ibid., p. 653.
[106]Andrist, p. 201.

CHAPTER V

[1]*Records of the War Department,* Consolidated Quartermaster Records, 1865-1882, Fort Dodge, Kansas, August 24, 1870. Hereafter cited as *Quartermaster Records.*
[2]Ibid., April 12, 1882.
[3]Ibid.
[4]Ibid.
[5]Ibid., May 26, 1875.
[6]Ibid., April 12, 1882.
[7]*Records of the War Department,* Headquarters, Department of the Missouri, Special Orders, Number 6, June 30, 1877. Hereafter cited as *Special Orders.*
[8]*Records of the War Department,* Letters Sent, 1866-1882, Fort Dodge, Kansas, July 18, 1877. Hereafter cited as *Letters Sent.*
[9]*Quartermaster Records,* May 26, 1875.
[10]*Records of the War Department,* Consolidated Medical Records, Weekly Report of Sick and Wounded, Fort Dodge, Kansas, May 1, 1880. Hereafter cited as *Medical Records.*
[11]*Dodge City Times,* (Dodge City), March 8, 1879, p. 2.
[12]*Special Orders,* Number 12, January 18, 1876.
[13]*Dodge City Times,* August 7, 1877, p. 2.
[14]*Letters Sent,* November 16, 1873.
[15]*Dodge City Times,* August 28, 1877, p. 1.
[16]Ibid., October 11, 1878, p. 3.
[17]Ibid., November 7, 1877, p. 1.
[18]Ibid., November 3, 1877, p. 8.
[19]Ibid., August 10, 1878, p. 1.
[20]Ibid., June 16, 1877, p. 5. The language of this article is Aesophian. The editor is undoubtedly chiding both the military and local citizenry for their frequent acts of violence.

CHAPTER V continued

[21]*Governor's Papers,* Archives, Kansas State Historical Society, Topeka, Colonel Richard I. Dodge to Governor Thomas Osborn, July 5, 1873. Hereafter cited as *Governor's Papers.*
[22]*Letters Sent,* February 20, 1876.
[23]*Dodge City Times,* April 27, 1877, p. 1.
[24]Ibid., August 10, 1878, p. 1.
[25]Ibid., October 28, 1877, p. 2.
[26]Ibid., June 26, 1877, p. 2.
[27]*Dodge City Daily Globe* (Dodge City), October 19, 1953, p. 4.
[28]*Dodge City Times,* July 20, 1877, p. 1.
[29]C. E. Campbell, "Down Among the Red Men," *Kansas Historical Collections* XVII (1926-1928), p. 673.
[30]*Letters Sent,* September 15, 1878.
[31]Ibid., September 7, 1878.
[32]Ibid., September 12, 1878.
[33]*Dodge City Times,* September 28, 1878.
[34]*Letters Sent,* September 12, 1878.
[35]Ibid., September 14, 1878.
[36]*Ford County Globe* (Dodge City), September 24, 1878, p. 2.
[37]*Letters Sent,* September 19, 1878.
[38]Ibid., September 18, 1878.
[39]George W. Brown, "Kansas Indian Wars," *Kansas Historical Collections,* XVII (1926-1928), p. 135.
[40]J. W. Berryman, "Early Settlement of Southwest Kansas," *Kansas Historical Collections,* VII (1926-1928), pp. 568-569.
[41]*Letters Sent,* September 27, 1878.
[42]Berryman, p. 570.
[43]*Dodge City Times,* September 28, 1878, p. 2.
[44]Ibid.
[45]Ibid., September 21, 1878, p. 2.
[46]*Governor's Papers,* Telegrams, James Kelly to Governor George T. Anthony, September 18, 1878.
[47]Ibid., Robert M. Wright to Governor George T. Anthony, November 22, 1878.
[48]*Letters Sent,* September 27, 1878.
[49]Brown, p. 136.
[50]Berryman, pp. 568-589.
[51]*Letters Sent,* September 29, 1878.
[52]Brown, p. 136.
[53]*Medical Records,* October 1, 1878.
[54]*Dodge City Times,* October 5, 1878, p. 2.
[55]Ralph K. Andrist, *The Long Death* (New York: Macmillan, 1964), p. 321.
[56]Ibid.
[57]*Dodge City Times,* November 30, 1878, p. 2.
[58]*Letters Sent,* September 15, 1878.
[59]Andrist, p. 324.
[60]*Dodge City Times,* November 23, 1878, p. 2.
[61]Andrist, p. 321.
[62]Ibid., pp. 321-322.
[63]*Dodge City Times,* November 30, 1878, p. 2.
[65]Ibid.
[66]Ibid., p. 326.
[67]Ibid., p. 327.
[68]*Dodge City Times,* February 22, 1879, p. 1.
[69]*Governor's Papers,* Michael W. Sutton to Governor Anthony, December 6, 1878.
[70]*Dodge City Times,* January 18, 1879, p. 2.
[71]Ibid.

CHAPTER V continued

[72]*Governor's Papers,* Michael W. Sutton to Governor St. John, January 15, 1879.
[73]Ibid., J. H. Hammond, United States Indian Inspector to Governor Anthony, December 6, 1878.
[74]Ibid., Michael W. Sutton to Governor St. John, February 11, 1879.
[75]*Dodge City Times,* February 22, 1879, p. 1.
[76]Ibid.
[77]Ibid.
[78]Ibid., February 8, 1879, p. 1.
[79]Ibid., February 22, 1879, p. 2.
[80]*Governor's Papers,* H. B. Johnson to Governor St. John, June 16, 1879.
[81]Ibid., William B. Masterson to Governor St. John, June 25, 1879.
[82]Ibid.
[83]Nyle H. Miller and Joseph W. Snell, *Why the West Was Wild* (Topeka: Jean M. Neibarger, 1963), p. 388.
[84]*House Executive Documents,* 45 Congress 2 Session, Number 78 (Serial 1809), pp. 4-7.
[85]Ibid.
[86]*Dodge City Times,* January 25, 1879, p. 3.
[87]*House Reports,* 46 Congress, 2 Session, Number 723, Bill Number 3191, pp. 1-3.
[88]*House Executive Documents,* 47 Congress, 1 Session, Number 195 (Serial 2031), pp. 1-5.
[89]George L. Anderson, "The Administration of Federal Land Laws in Western Kansas, 1880-1890: A Factor in Adjustment to a New Environment," *Kansas Historical Quarterly,* XX (November, 1952), p. 249.
[90]*Senate Executive Documents,* 51 Congress, 1 Session, Number 73 (Serial 2686), p. 6.
[91]*Special Orders,* Number 51, April 5, 1882.
[92]Ibid., Number 168, October 2, 1882.

EPILOGUE

[1]*House Executive Documents,* 47 Congress, First Session, (Serial 225), p. 7.
[2]*Records of the War Department,* Office of the Adjutant General, Report on Abandoned Forts, March 17, 1883.
[3]Robert M. Wright, *Dodge City the Cowboy Capital,* Wichita: The Wichita Eagle Press, 1913, p. 328.
[4]Leo E. Oliva, "Soldiers Along the Santa Fe Trail," unpublished M. A. Thesis, Denver University.
[5]Ibid., August 10, 1886, p. 2.
[6]*United States Statutes at Large,* XXIII, pp. 103-104.
[7]*Senate Executive Documents,* 49 Congress, First Session, (Serial 98), p. 1.
[8]*Congressional Record,* 50 Congress, Second Session, Part 3, p. 2326.
[9]*United States Statutes at Large,* XV, p. 1012.
[10]*Senate Executive Documents,* 51 Congress, First Session, (Serial 73), pp. 6-7.
[11]*House Executive Documents,* 47 Congress, First Session, (Serial 2031), pp. 2-7.
[12]*Records of Admissions and Military History of Members of the Kansas State Soldier's Home,* February 7, 1890-May 31, 1901, Volume 1, p. 1.
[13]*Kansas Soldier's Home, Rules and Regulations,* Office of the State Printer, Topeka, Kansas, August 1, 1960, p. 1.
[14]Ibid., p. 2.
[15]*Records of Admissions and Military History of Members of the Kansas State Soldier's Home,* February 7, 1890-May 31, 1901, Volume I, p. 1.
[16]Ibid., pp. 1-20.
[17]Ibid., p. 15.
[18]Ibid., pp. 1-198.
[19]Ibid., pp. 1-19.
[20]Ibid., pp. 1-198.

EPILOGUE continued

[21]Ibid., p. 1.
[22]Ibid., p. 5.
[23]Ibid., p. 12.
[24]Ibid., p. 13.
[25]Ibid., pp. 1-198.
[26]Ibid., p. 18.
[27]Ibid., pp. 1-36.
[28]*Records of Deaths and Burials at Kansas State Soldier's Home,* 1890-1969, p. 7.
[29]Ibid., p. 43.
[30]Ibid., Records of Admissions, Volume II, p. 103.
[31]Personal Interview with Arthur Rose, Superintendent, Kansas State Soldier's Home, March 19, 1969.
[32]Personal Interview with Thomas North, resident of Kansas State Soldier's Home, March 20, 1969.
[33]Personal Interview with Edward P. Mann, Veteran of Spanish-American War and resident of Kansas State Soldier's Home, March 20, 1969.
[34]Personal Interview with Arthur Rose, March 19, 1969.

BIBLIOGRAPHY

PRIMARY BOOKS AND MEMOIRS

Crawford, Samuel J. *Kansas in the Sixties.* Chicago: A. C. McClurg and Company, 1911.

Dodge, Major General Grenville M. *The Battle of Atlanta and other Campaigns, Addresses, Etc.* Council Bluffs, Iowa: The Monarch Printing Company, 1911.

Dodge, Richard Irving. *Plains of the Great West.* New York: Archer House, Inc., 1959.

Sheridan, General Philip H. *Records of Engagements with Hostile Indians within the Military Division of the Missouri from 1868 to 1882.* Chicago: Headquarters Military Division of the Missouri, 1882.

Stanley, Henry M. *My Early Travels and Adventures in America and Asia.* London: Sampson Low, Marston and Company, Volume I, 1895.

Wright, Robert M. *Dodge City the Cowboy Capital.* Wichita: The Wichita Eagle Press, 1913.

GOVERNMENT PUBLICATIONS AND RECORDS

United States. Department of War. *The War of the Rebellion: A Compilation of the Union and Confederate Armies.* Volumes 1, 2, 3, 8, 22, 28, 34, 41, 48, 53. Washington: Government Printing Office, 1880-1901.

United States. *House Executive Document Number 1.* Fortieth Congress, Third Session (Serial 1367), Washington: Government Printing Office, 1892.

United States. *House Executive Document, Report of Secretary of War,* Forty-first Congress, Second Session (Serial 1412), Washington: Government Printing Office, 1892.

United States. *House Executive Document Number 1,* Forty-second Congress, Third Session (Serial 1558), Washington: Government Printing Office, 1892.

United States. *House Executive Document Numbers 195 and 225,* Forty-seventh Congress, First Session (Serial 2031), Washington: Government Printing Office, 1892.

United States. *House Reports Number 723,* Forty-sixth Congress, Second Session (Bill Number 3191), Washington: Government Printing Office, 1892.

United States. *Senate Executive Document Number 13,* Fortieth Congress, First Session (Serial 1308), Washington: Government Printing Office, 1892.

United States. *Senate Executive Document Number 73,* Fifty-first Congress, First Session (Serial 2686), Washington: Government Printing Office, 1892.

United States. *Congressional Record Part 3,* Fiftieth Congress, Second Session, Washington: Government Printing Office, 1892.

United States. *Records of the War Department,* Post Returns, Fort Dodge, Kansas 1866-1882.

United States. *Records of the War Department,* Circular Number 4, Surgeon General's Office, Report on Barracks and Hospitals, with Descriptions of Military Posts.

United States. *Records of the War Department,* Consolidated Medical Records, Fort Dodge, Kansas, 1865-1882.

United States. *Records of the War Department,* Reports and Journals of Scouts and Marches, Fort Dodge, Kansas, 1867-1879.

United States. *Records of the War Department,* Special Orders, Fort Dodge, Kansas, 1866-1882.

United States. *Records of the War Department,* Office of Adjutant General, Record Group 94, Post Returns, Fort Atchison, Kansas.

United States. *Records of the War Department,* Telegrams Received, Fort Dodge, Kansas, 1874.

United States. *Records of the War Department,* Consolidated Quartermaster Records, Fort Dodge, Kansas, 1865-1882.

United States. *Records of the War Department,* Letters Sent, Fort Dodge, Kansas, 1866-1882.

United States. *Records of the War Department,* Orders and General Orders, Fort Dodge, Kansas, 1866-1882.

United States. *Records of the War Department,* Letters Sent, Fort Harker, Kansas, 1864-1875.

United States. *Records of the War Department,* General Field Orders, Number 1, Headquarters, Department of the Missouri, 1867.

United States. *Records of the War Department,* Military Division of the Missouri, Contract Number 2776, July 9, 1873.

United States. *Records of the War Department,* Office of Adjutant General, Report on Abandoned Forts, 1882.

State of Kansas. *Records of Admissions and Military History,* Members of Kansas State Soldier's Home, Fort Dodge, Kansas, I and II, February 7, 1890-May 31,1901.

State of Kansas. *Records of Deaths and Burials,* Kansas State Soldier's Home, Fort Dodge, Kansas, 1890-1969.

State of Kansas. *Kansas Soldier's Home,* Rules and Regulations, Topeka: Office of the State Printer, August 1, 1960.

State of Kansas. *Governor's Papers,* Letters and Telegrams, Archives, Kansas State Historical Society, Topeka, Kansas.

State of Kansas. *Drawing 189,* Kansas, 8-3, Military Reservations, Fort Dodge, Kansas, Archives, Kansas State Historical Society, Topeka, Kansas.

State of Kansas. *Letter:* General Grenville M. Dodge to Joseph B. Thoburn, October 24, 1910, Archives, Kansas State Historical Society, Topeka, Kansas.

State of Kansas. *Treaty of the Little Arkansas,* Official Copy, Archives, Kansas State Historical Society, Topeka, Kansas.

State of Kansas. *Treaty of Medicine Lodge Creek,* Official Copy, Archives, Kansas State Historical Society, Topeka, Kansas.

United States. *United States Statutes at Large,* XXIII, XV.

SECONDARY BOOKS

Andrist, Ralph K. *The Long Death.* New York: Macmillan, 1964.

Billington, Ray Allen. *The Far Western Frontier, 1830-1860.* New York: Harper Brothers, 1956.

Billington, Ray Allen. *Westward Expansion: A History of the American Frontier.* New York: Macmillan, 1960.

Castel, Albert. *A Frontier State at War: Kansas, 1861-1865.* Ithaca: Cornell University Press, 1958.

Forsyth, Brigadier General George A. *The Story of the Soldier.* New York: D. Appleton and Company, 1905.

Frazer, Robert W. *Forts of the West.* Norman: University of Oklahoma Press, 1965.

Grinnell, George Bird. *The Fighting Cheyennes.* New York: Charles Scribner's Sons, 1915.

Krumrey, Kate W. *Saga of the Sawlog.* Denver: Big Mountain Press, 1965.

Miller, Nyle H. and Snell, Joseph W. *Why The West Was Wild.* Topeka: Jean M. Neibarger, 1963.

Oliva, Leo E. *Soldiers on the Santa Fe Trail, 1829-1880.* Norman: University of Oklahoma Press, 1967.

Prentis, Noble L. *A History of Kansas.* Topeka: Caroline Prentis, 1909.

Ricky, Don Jr. *Forty Miles A Day on Beans and Hay: The Enlisted Soldier Fighting the Indian Wars.* Norman: University of Oklahoma Press, 1962.

Rister, Carl C. *Border Command: General Phil Sheridan in the West.* Norman: University of Oklahoma Press, 1944.

Walker, Henry P. *The Wagonmasters: High Plains Freighting from the Earliest Days of the Santa Fe Trail to 1880.* Norman: University of Oklahoma Press, 1957.

Webb, Walter Prescott. *The Great Plains.* Boston: Ginn and Company, 1959.

Welmann, Paul I. *Death on the Prairie: The Thirty Years Struggle for the Western Plains.* New York: Macmillan.

Winther, Oscar Osburn. *The Transportation Frontier: Trans-Mississippi West, 1865-1890.* New York: Holt, Rinehart and Winston, 1964.

Vestal, Stanley. *The Old Santa Fe Trail.* Boston: Houghton Mifflin Company, 1939.

Zornow, William F. *Kansas: A History of the Jayhawk State.* Norman: University of Oklahoma Press, 1959.

PERIODICALS

Anderson, George L. "The Administration of Federal Land Laws in Western Kansas, 1880-1890: A Factor in Adjustment to a New Envrionment." *Kansas Historical Quarterly,* XX (November, 1952), 233-251.

Berryman, J. W. "Early Settlement of Southwest Kansas." *Kansas Historical Collections,* VII (1926-28), 561-570.

Brewerton, George D. "In the Buffalo Country," *Harper's Magazine.* XXIV (June, 1862), 457.

Brown, George W. "Kansas Indian Wars." *Kansas Historical Collections,* XVII (1926-28), 134-139.

Campbell, C. E. "Down Among the Red Men." *Kansas Historical Collections,* XVII (1926-28), 623-691.

Connelley, William E. "The Treaty Held at Medicine Lodge." *Kansas Historical Collections,* XVII (1926-28), 601-606.

Davis, Theodore. "Winter on the Plains." *Harper's Magazine,* XXXIX (June, 1869), 24.

Fite, Gilbert C. "The United States Army and Relief to Pioneer Settlers, 1874-1875." *Journal of the West,* VI (January, 1967), 99-107.

Garfield, Marvin. "Defense of the Kansas Frontier, 1864-1865." *Kansas Historical Quarterly,* I (February, 1932), 140-152.

Garfield, Marvin. "Defense of the Kansas Frontier, 1868-1869." *Kansas Historical Quarterly,* I (November, 1932), 451-473.

Garfield, Marvin. "The Military Post as a Factor in the Frontier Defense of Kansas, 1865-1869." *Kansas Historical Quarterly,* I (November, 1931), 50-62.

Karnes, Thomas L. "Gilpin's Volunteers on the Santa Fe Trail." *Kansas Historical Quarterly,* XXX (September, 1964), 1-14.

Lewis, Theodore R. "A Summer on the Plains." *Harper's Magazine,* XXXVI (May, 1868), 295.

Moore, Horace L. "The Nineteenth Kansas Cavalry." *Kansas Historical Collections,* VI (1897-1900), 35-52.

Nichols, Colonel George Ward. "The Indian: What We Should Do With Him." *Harper's Magazine,* XV (June, 1870), 732-739.

Runyon, A. L. "A. L. Runyon's Letters from the Nineteenth Kansas Regiment." *Kansas Historical Quarterly,* IX (1940), 58-75.

Unrau, William E. "Indian Agent vs the Army: Some Background Notes on the Kiowa-Comanche Treaty of 1865." *Kansas Historical Quarterly,* XXX (Summer, 1964), 129-152.

Weichselbaum, Theodore. "Statement of Theodore Weichselbaum of Ogden, Riley County, July 17, 1908." *Kansas Historical Collections,* XI (1909-1910), 561-571.

White, Lonnie J. "Winter Campaigning with Sheridan and Custer: The Expedition of the 19th Kansas Volunteer Cavalry." *Journal of the West,* VI (January, 1967), 76.

Wyman, Walker D. "The Military Phase of Santa Fe Freighting, 1846-1865." *Kansas Historical Quarterly,* I (1931-32), 415-428.

NEWSPAPERS

Dodge City Daily Globe (Dodge City, Kansas), December 24, 1934-October 19, 1953.
Dodge City Times (Dodge City, Kansas), June 1, 1877-June 28, 1882.
Ford County Globe (Dodge City, Kansas), October 24, 1878.
Junction City Union (Junction City, Kansas), September 30, 1865-June 19, 1879.
Kansas Weekly Herald (Leavenworth, Kansas), March 2, 1855-June 14, 1856.
The Smoky Hill and Republican Union (Junction City, Kansas), April 4, 1862-October 8, 1864.
The Western Journal of Commerce (St. Louis, Missouri), June 11, 1863-October 21, 1865.
Weekly Osage Chronicle (Burlingame, Kansas), August 27, 1864-August 28, 1868.

INTERVIEWS

Mann, Edward P., Veteran of Spanish-American War, Resident of Kansas State Soldier's Home, Fort Dodge, Kansas, personal interview, March 20, 1969, with author.
North, Thomas, Resident of Kansas State Soldier's Home, Fort Dodge, Kansas, personal interview, March 20, 1969, with author.
Rose, Arthur, Superintendent, Kansas State Soldier's Home, Fort Dodge, Kansas, personal interview, March 19, 1969, with author.

INDEX

Few geographical regions have been endowed with the rich and colorful cultural legacy that is descriptive of Western Kansas during the frontier days. The restless explorer, the curious and often exploited Redman, the dutiful soldier and the hopeful settler, all converged on the area as America's frontier experience pressed forward.

Far too often the irreplaceable details and instruments of this period have been lost. With the passage of time memories grow dim and "oldtimers" pass on. Objects and manuscripts whose historical value have not been established are discarded. As the fiber of the past is forfeited posterity is denied the opportunity of sharing yesterday.

The federal government has responded to this steady attrition by creating the Cultural Heritage and Arts Center at Dodge City, Kansas; a unique and ambitious project dedicated to preserving our national experience.

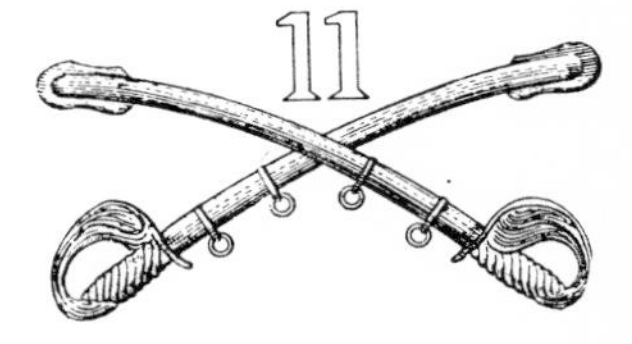